HAUNTED
CHARLESTON

HAUNTED CHARLESTON

Scary Sites, Eerie Encounters, and Tall Tales

Retold by Sara Pitzer

Guilford, Connecticut

Text design: Sheryl P. Kober
Editor: Meredith Dias
Project editor: Lauren Szalkiewicz
Layout: Lisa Reneson, Two Sisters Design

Library of Congress Cataloging-in-Publication Data

Pitzer, Sara.
 Haunted Charleston : scary sites, eerie encounters, and tall tales /
Retold by Sara Pitzer. — [First edition].
 pages cm
 ISBN 978-0-7627-7182-0

1. Haunted places—South Carolina—Charleston. 2. Ghosts—
South Carolina—Charleston. I. Title.
 BF1472.U6P585 2013
 133.109757'915—dc23
                                          2012050346

Printed in the United States of America

Distributed by NATIONAL BOOK NETWORK

This is for the skeptics.
Their challenges make telling the stories fun.

CONTENTS

ACKNOWLEDGMENTS

Good editors keep authors from looking like idiots. I have been fortunate to work with some of the best, most literate editors on this project. I owe thanks to former Globe Pequot Press editor Meredith Rufino, who got me into this in the first place. Meredith Dias helped me make the chapters sound like stories, not history lessons. Project editor Lauren Szalkiewicz kept things moving from one stage to another and offered suggestions when I got stuck on how to express an idea. Copy editor Jessie Shiers caught inconsistencies, misused words and typos, and, here's a biggie, she pointed out that six and four did not add up to eleven, even in a ghost story. I appreciated cover designer Bret Kerr's invitation to suggest picture ideas for the *Haunted Charleston* cover and then to actually use one, as well as letting me see the results ahead of time. Believe me, that doesn't always happen in publishing. And it was all done with good humor and patience. My thanks to each of you, individually and as a team.

Of course the manuscript would never have gotten to Globe Pequot Press at all without ongoing help and advice from the IT team at Innovative Solutions in Albemarle, North Carolina. These people fix problems and make it look easy, and being around them is so much fun I occasionally stop in just for a mood lift.

Finally, a word for all the friends who smile when I stomp around insisting I'll never write another book. Just you wait, guys. You'll see.

INTRODUCTION

In Charleston, many of the people who live in old houses will tell you that they have a ghost, sometimes more than one. These haunted residents say they've become so used to the company that they don't think much about it. It makes sense to them that people who once lived in a fine old home they loved should return to it in spirit after dying. Because these are almost always friendly hauntings, their experiences seldom develop into full-fledged stories. Instead, they are just part of household lore. These are not the folks who write books or conduct tours or grant interviews; they just take it as part of daily life—no threat and no big talking point, either.

It takes the storytellers to develop a good ghost tale. The guides who narrate ghost tours in Charleston often tell their groups that you need two things to have ghosts: dead people and dramatic history. Charleston has it all. Conflict and war, natural disasters, personal tragedy, wickedness, and cruelty have spawned Charleston's ghost stories for centuries. The nickname "Holy City" comes not because the settlers were particularly saintly but because they established churches of every denomination when they arrived.

The city's stories continue to change as they are passed from one generation to another. Back when the ghostly tales in Charleston were only an oral tradition, the details and emphasis of a story varied from one storyteller to the next. Capturing the stories in writing added new dimension to the anecdotes by giving them a different kind of permanence. John Bennett's book *The Doctor to the Dead*, first published in 1943, is a collection of tales based on folklore from the

Gullah tradition. When Bennett began working on his book, he found that the old stories were disappearing, and he often had to talk to many sources to piece together one full narrative, allowing himself some invention when he couldn't get enough detail.

In the late 1960s, Nancy Rhyne began collecting ghost stories that had been in the oral tradition of descendants of emancipated slaves, both through interviews and reviewing Works Progress Administration (WPA) documents. Similarly, Margaret Rhett Martin began gathering Charleston ghost stories, many of which were published first in the Columbia, South Carolina, newspaper *The State,* then later revised and expanded in her book *Charleston Ghosts.* New versions of Lowcountry ghost stories, including mine, owe credit to the writers who've worked before us—and, of course, to those early storytellers who spun tales by the fireplace or around a campfire on long evenings, well before radio or television.

The electronic world has added yet another dimension to our knowledge of ghostly happenings. The Internet and YouTube carry personal accounts of experiences that could have happened as recently as yesterday, and, especially around Halloween, television stations in the region inevitably send reporters and camera operators to allegedly haunted sites to talk with people about what they've seen and experienced. Their accounts are immediate and personal (whether invented or real) and often breathe new life into old legends.

In Charleston, local authors Ed Macy and Julian T. Buxton III have developed the idea of verifying a haunting by interviewing people who have had similar ghostly experiences at the same place. Their book, *The Ghosts of Charleston*, published in 2001, contains stories based on their interviews plus documented background history to explain the details.

Another development in exploring unexplained hauntings is the increasing number of people who specialize in paranormal investigation, either professionally or as amateurs. For them, Charleston is a hot spot. These individuals usually work as teams, sometimes using an astounding variety of devices to measure magnetic fields, sounds, ultraviolet light, motion, etc. They often post detailed reports of what they've experienced on the Internet. In Charleston, the Old Jail, for example, has been the subject of intense study by Joshua Warren and his group, the League of Energy Materialization and Unexplained phenomena Research (LEMUR). Their findings indicate, at the very least, that something unexplained often happens at the jail.

For all the storytelling, scientific testing, and observing, some of the most famous unexplained manifestations in Charleston have been captured by amateur photographers who weren't even trying. A tourist walking by the house at Poogan's Porch snapped a picture of a second-story window covered by a lace curtain. The picture shows the shadowy, but unmistakable, image of a woman's face in the window. And a local man winding up a day of photographing architecture snapped a few pictures in the fading evening light at the St. Philip's graveyard. One of his photos, now widely distributed, shows the pale figure of a woman kneeling at the gravestone of a child buried with its mother more than a hundred years ago. Kodak inspected the film and assured the man that his photo hadn't been tampered with.

Nor can we discount the experiences of various guests who have stayed at the 1837 Bed and Breakfast, where a ghost seems to want to join them in their rooms. Here it's good to distinguish between malevolent and benevolent spirits. The malevolent ones may interact with humans by scratching, pinching, or pushing, for instance, while a benevolent spirit just wants to be friends. Other apparitions don't appear at all aware of living people around them. While the ghosts at 1836 Meeting Street seem friendly, for example, those at the Old Jail don't, and those wandering about Dock Street Theatre show no sign of noticing anyone. In Charleston you can take your pick.

Ghosts have become big business in Charleston. Nobody is sure who came up with the title "Most Haunted City"; it might have been either historians or the chamber of commerce. When one tourist commented on that title, a tour guide said, "It's not that we have more ghosts than anywhere else. We just do a better job of marketing them." Oddly enough, the proprietors of lodgings said to be haunted used to try to keep it quiet for fear of losing business. Now, a ghost or two seems to attract guests. The more you learn about the city's history, the easier it is to believe that, for whatever reason, spirits still hang around. They come from the city's earliest days of pirates and colonists, the later revolution against England, the Civil War, city-wide fires, and ongoing weather disasters.

Julian Buxton, who established a ghost tour company with Ed Macy, wrote in *The Ghosts of Charleston* that he once felt so haunted by ghosts in Charleston that he moved away. Getting into the ghost business, so to speak, made it easier for him to come home. John Harden, a North Carolina journalist who wrote accounts of supernatural experiences as they were told to him, said that the longer he worked with such stories, the more he became aware of unseen presences.

He didn't mind; they didn't seem to want anything from him or to cause harm in any way.

It all comes down to this: No matter where you fall on the continuum from skepticism to belief, the stories persist and evolve. Sometimes skeptics meet a spirit in Charleston that scares them, while believers may go away wondering why they haven't had a spooky experience. One tour guide says it is often the skeptics who have encounters that leave them believing in ghosts—and not always eager to repeat the experience.

Part One

HOSPITALITY HAUNTS

Rumors that some of the lodgings and eateries in the Carolinas are haunted have circulated almost from the moment they opened for business. For years, owners tried to suppress the stories for fear they would keep people from patronizing their hostelries and restaurants, assuming that a scary experience was the last thing a customer on vacation would want. But, of course, the stories got around anyway, and as they did, the mood shifted. Magazines published stories about inns' resident ghosts, and people booked reservations specifically to meet them. As interest mounted, books began to appear containing listings only of haunted places to eat and sleep. People bought them. Inevitably, seeing a new trend in the hospitality business, owners began promoting the ghost stories of their properties instead of suppressing them, and now some places even publicize their hauntings on their websites.

Chapter 1
Spooky Full House

Battery Carriage House Inn
20 South Battery Street

The house at 20 South Battery Street was built in 1843. It changed hands a number of times before Drayton Hastie bought the mansion and opened its carriage house as a bed-and-breakfast inn in 1976. Since then it has come to be known as Charleston's most haunted inn. The two most frequent sightings reported are a headless male torso and a young, well-dressed man.

The Battery Carriage House Inn has eleven guest rooms, but so many ghosts hang around the place that you almost wonder if there's room for guests. Apparently, they share the space. Visitors have recorded so many strange experiences in the guest books that Hastie has compiled them and posted them on the Internet (www.batterycarriagehouse .com/ghosts.htm). The travel blogs pay more attention to the amenities of the place: four-poster beds, lush gardens, and turndown service in the evening.

Travelers who stay in room 8 typically report charm and comfort in a "simply but nicely appointed room." They like "breakfast served on a silver tray in your room or the rose garden." A modern steam shower gets enthusiastic mentions. And a couple celebrating their fifteenth wedding anniversary was tickled to find a bottle of champagne in the room.

But some folks report more frightening experiences. The headless ghost of a burly, growling, threatening man visits in the middle of the night. A man and his wife who were staying at the inn for the first time wrote that the staff was lovely and hospitable, with an atmosphere that transported them back to a time when the pace of living was slower. It was, as usual, the wife who took the trouble to write in the guest book. She wanted to talk about the ghost.

According to her account, she and her husband stayed in room 8. She described herself as "a believer" and her husband as a skeptic. Both of them, however, had a restless night. The husband kept waking up because he felt someone hovering over him. His wife saw and took pictures of orbs and dancing lights in the room. She even went outside while her husband slept to take more pictures, including some from the courtyard, facing the door of their room. Then, at about 2:00 a.m., a scary, loud noise—like something being slammed into a wall in the bathroom—woke up the skeptical husband again, and at this point he got his wife to look around with him. They didn't see a thing. Mrs. Believer's story doesn't end there, though. After she got home and uploaded the pictures she'd taken to her computer, she saw what looked like a man's headless torso outside the room, as well as several clear shots of the unexplained orbs and lights in the room. Believer or not, she wasn't scared, and she wrote to Hastie that they'd be back for the soft sheets, delicious breakfast, friendly staff, and good air-conditioning.

But other guests have had experiences they aren't anxious to repeat. (It is one thing to see a ghost, quite another to touch one.) One man and his wife went to sleep in room 8 without giving it much thought. Haunting wasn't a concept they took seriously. When he awoke with a sense of being watched, the man might have dismissed it as a dream—even though he was seeing the torso of a burly man with no head, arms, or legs hovering at the end of the bed, breathing heavily and moaning. The man thought it was probably some kind of picture the innkeepers projected to meet the ghostly expectations of bed-and-breakfast guests, but when it didn't go away, he reached toward the apparition's torso. He felt his arm go right through it and stick there, as if the ghost didn't want him to let go. In the course of managing to wiggle free, he felt a coarse wool fabric and his arm got cold. The ghost made a growling sound and disappeared.

According to many, this is the spirit of a Confederate soldier ordered to stay toward the end of the Siege of Charleston and blow up munitions left behind by fleeing soldiers and families. That way, the Federals could not turn the Confederacy's own munitions against them. The building, which later became the inn, had been used as temporary accommodations for nine Confederate soldiers—one of whom was blown up by the explosives the soldiers were trying to destroy.

But the ghost's coarse wool clothing leads some to speculate that the visitor was a pirate hanged at the Battery point, where hangings of captured pirates were common. Whoever he is—or was—this guy is not friendly now. Some guests in room 8 have reported the blinds closing by themselves and sticking so they cannot be opened again. All who have experienced the unexplained phenomena in room 8 agree that while they've not been harmed by the visiting (or perhaps resident) spirit, they've felt threatened by him.

The haunt of room 10 seems to be a much sweeter, nicely dressed presence who likes to be near the ladies. His story is a romance that didn't work out. He was engaged to marry his local sweetheart, but he agreed to his parents' wish that first he go off to study at Yale University. It happens often enough; romances fall apart when going off to college separates a couple.

In this story, it happened in a hurry. Just a week after her fiancé headed off for higher education, the young woman ran away to marry a boy who had stayed home. Long before the days of iPhones and fast communication, the young man's parents decided to spare him the sad news until he came home. Maybe somewhere in New Haven, Connecticut, their son would meet a young woman more suited to their social status and his education. As many parents know, children often don't fulfill family hopes. So it developed with the young Yale scholar. When he arrived in Charleston during a break, eager to see his sweetheart and never having even thought of another girl, his parents had to tell him that she'd married someone else.

In a sense, you could say he died of a broken heart. He dressed in his nicest suit, climbed to the roof of what is now the inn, and jumped. Some say this was the house where his parents lived at the time and he meant to punish them with his death there; others believe he worked at this house when he was home to earn money for college and just wanted a familiar place to end his misery. Now, as resident ghost, the tall, slender young man seems to be looking for his lost love. Could it be that his extreme gesture was a final declaration to his parents that he would remain faithful to his first love forever, in this life and the next? Or is he now looking for a new love? As a ghost, he does like the ladies, and he is sweet to them.

Take the story of the twin sisters, for instance. One of them was asleep, while the other lay still awake. The sister who was awake saw a nicely dressed young man materialize through a wall and lie down next to her on the bed. When she tried to wake her sister to show her, the apparition stood up, gave a courtly little bow, and left the same way he'd come in. He might have been looking for one girlfriend, but not two. He had been a gentleman once, after all. According to other reports, any time a woman expresses alarm when he lies down next to her, he leaves immediately—through a wall, of course.

Sometimes the spirit may get confused about whether the lady in the room is already "taken." Alan Brown writes the story in *Ghosts and Strange Phenomena of the Palmetto State* about a couple who booked room 10 to celebrate a wedding anniversary. The wife was stretched out on the bed watching television while her husband was downstairs talking to Cathy Jo Connor, the concierge, about how to spend the next day. The woman was distracted from the TV program by a shadow passing outside the window, and then by the scent of an unfamiliar cologne—something like Old Spice, definitely not what her husband used—at the same time the shadow came into the room. She got scared and ran to open the door. The shadow disappeared immediately, at the same time that her husband was coming up the stairs to their room. The couple went ahead with their plans to spend the night, and nothing more happened. Later, they wrote a note to the innkeeper about the experience and also said that they liked the inn. Unlike the haint of room 8, the ghost of room 10 is a fully formed body, with arms, legs, and head intact, though his facial features are undefined.

While these are the two most distinctive ghostly personalities at the inn, they aren't the only signs of paranormal activity. The Ghostly Congregation, as it has come to be called, is a collection of unexplained activities that puzzle inn guests in room 3. Sometimes cell phones that are turned off chirp and flash, although there is no signal in the guest room. When that happens, the bathroom faucet starts to drip. Also at night, a large blob of light sometimes floats from one room to another, and people see shapes that appear to be energy masses of various sizes moving around the room, congregating like a group of people. This room used to be part of the wine cellar, as likely a meeting place for otherworld spirits as any.

One guest awoke in the early hours of the morning and saw the interior shutters of room 3's door moving. Shutters opening from rooms into other parts of a house were once the only way to provide ventilation, and even though modern air conditioners keep rooms cool now, the shutters are still part of many structures. In this case, the activity seemed almost rhythmic. As Mr. Hastie described it, "First it was the top shutter. After a few moments, the two bottom shutters started moving at the same time. Then the top two shutters. A shadow moved over just the top two sets without casting a shadow over the bottom two. Next, the bottom left shutter closed, then the bottom right, then the top left, leaving only the top right open." The guest turned on a bathroom light so that the room would not be completely dark no matter what happened, but nothing more did after that. In the morning, when she mentioned the experience to her husband, he said he'd seen a ghostly human face in the mirror. The face quickly disappeared, and the husband went back to sleep. Mr. Hastie writes that neither the man nor his wife had known the inn was haunted. Of course, word has gotten around now.

Guests aren't the only people to experience odd events at Battery Carriage House. Sometimes in rooms 8 and 10, the housekeepers get soaking wet when the showers they are trying to clean turn on full force by themselves. No, the housekeepers insist, they could not have turned them on accidentally. They clean showers all the time. They know how to do it without turning the water on themselves.

Terrance Zepke, the author of *Best Ghost Tales of South Carolina*, had a series of unnerving experiences when she met a television production crew at the Battery Carriage House to tape an interview about hauntings. Although it was July, an extremely hot and muggy time of year in Charleston, Zepke shivered and felt cold when she got to the notorious room 10, where the television broadcast equipment had been set up for the interview. The hair on her arms stood up. This is a phenomenon often reported by paranormal investigators working in a spot where they don't actually see anything— at least, not right away. When the broadcast crew did a final check of their equipment before the interview, they found that the lights had been changed from the way they'd first been set up and had to be reset. Then, some of the lights abruptly burned out, even though they were not old.

After that, the interview went on without further complication, except for some distortion at the end of the tape. When the job was over, the crew packed up their equipment quickly. Zepke didn't exactly run away, but she didn't loiter, either. Any of them might return to the eleven-room inn for further investigation, but you probably couldn't get Zepke or the crew to sleep in rooms 8 or 10. All that paranormal activity might make it a nice place to visit if you're seeking a thrill, but you sure wouldn't want to live there.

Chapter 2
George's Playground

The 1837 Bed and Breakfast
126 Wentworth Street

Long before the house at 126 Wentworth Street became a bed-and-breakfast, it was a newly built home with a room on the third floor housing a slave couple and their nine-year-old son, George. Apparently, the spirit that stayed after his death never really grew up. People report that his ghost hangs around the old house, playing jokes on guests in the inn.

Maria just wanted a nap. A day of walking the streets of Charleston in June heat and humidity will do that to you. A late afternoon nap before heading out to enjoy some Low-country cuisine in one of the city's fabulous restaurants was just what she needed. But every time she dozed off, the sound of the chair rocking just outside her door jarred her awake. A polite request would probably be enough to get the lively rocker to stop. B&B guests tend to be considerate of one another. But when she looked out the window, the chair was empty. Rocking, but empty. Just then, the inn manager came to the bottom of the stairs and yelled, "Stop!" The rocking stopped. No big deal, in the manager's view. "Just George, playing again." In their book, *Haunted Charleston,* Ed Macy and Geordie Buxton attribute the story to an entry written in the bed-and-breakfast guestbook in 1999.

There've been lots of similar stories, before and since that entry. Events that triggered the stories date back to

1837, when the house was built. The building is a three-story, Federal-style single house. Charleston has many such structures, so called because they were built just one room wide, usually with stairs to the upper floors outside the building, and covered piazzas on the two long sides. (Piazza is Charleston speak for "porch.") These houses were set with the narrow end facing the street and the long piazzas facing the lawns, angled to catch as much cooling breeze as possible.

These days, guests at the 1837 Bed and Breakfast may stay in the house or in a carriage house room. Guests indulge in extravagant breakfasts each morning and take tea on the piazza later in the day. The rooms in the house impress guests with restored crown molding, wainscoting, high ceilings adorned with ceiling medallions, and the added benefit of modern amenities such as air-conditioning and minifridges.

It wouldn't have been quite so comfortable back in the day. The third floor, where the slave family lived, was probably hot. And unless they were working, George's parents wouldn't have spent time on the cooler piazzas. George worked in the stable on the property, sometimes ran errands, and found time to play along the banks of the Ashley River. As slaves' lives went at the time, it wasn't bad, especially for a little boy who liked to run in the grass, toss stones into the water, and watch other children play.

But it didn't last. The homeowner came on hard times and sold George's mother and father to a wealthy planter for a large sum of money. If he had been the owner of a big plantation, finances would not have deteriorated as seriously as they did for citizens limited to small properties in town. Slave families on large plantations were less likely to be broken up by such sales, although it did happen from time to time. George may have witnessed the transaction, during which his parents demonstrated their woodworking and weaving skills, were bought, paid for, and taken away by their new owner. After that, he would have had no choice but to return to the house on Wentworth Street with his owner—and without his parents.

So what would a nine-year-old kid who had lost his parents and did not know what was happening to them do? According to one story, George learned that his parents were aboard a slave ship in the Charleston Harbor and stole a rowboat so he could get to the ship and join his parents. The boat capsized and George drowned. Now his spirit hangs around the place where he last saw his mother and father, waiting for them to come back.

But maybe it didn't happen that way at all. A more realistic and better documented story is that George ran away, got caught somewhere outside Charleston, and was brought back and confined in one of Charleston's many barracoons. Barracoons were buildings used to house slaves about to be put up for auction. George wasn't for sale, but where else could officials put a young slave until they found his owner?

The conditions in the barracoon would have been awful. The Old Slave Mart at 6 Chalmers Street, now maintained as a museum by the city of Charleston, is an example of the typical barracoon. The buildings had rooms where potential buyers could talk to the enslaved men and women, as well as a balcony from which the slaves were displayed on auction day. Slaves were placed high on a balcony so that any flaws in their appearance would not be visible from the street. When displays and auctions were not going on, the enslaved could be chained hand and foot to the basement floor and walls. Even though he was still a boy, George might have been chained that way.

The next day his owner came for him, hauled him bodily from the building onto the carriage, and took him "home" to 126 Wentworth Street, where he went back to working in the stables. When George's owner came, he probably was carrying a bullwhip. Bullwhips were a standard part of life at the time, used to motivate and control slaves as well as animals. The whips were large and heavy and made a frightful noise when cracked. The phrase "crack the whip," used these days to suggest keeping people in line, probably came from those early times. If George's owner never used the whip on humans, it still might have been part of stable discipline. The unforgettable sound would have both motivated and frightened his slaves. George probably lived the rest of his life working in and around the stables hearing that sound every day.

It might have been a short life. Nobody really knows when or how George died because records of slaves were sometimes sparse, except for information about when and where they were purchased and for how much. It seems likely that a young slave, missing family care and company, might have died young, perhaps of loneliness or while trying again to escape to find his parents. He probably never did.

Even though nobody has actually seen his ghost, people say George is still around the only home he ever had, where, for a while, he was happy as a boy. The unseen spirit is so lively and full of mischief that people who encounter it say it must be a kid. Moreover, since it would be hard to discipline a ghost, George can do pretty much whatever he feels like doing. Over the years guests and employees at the bed-and-breakfast have reported lots of activity in and around the third-floor space, where George and his parents would have lived. Some of the mysterious events happen in the daytime. Doors spring open and, when closed, open again. Lights that were turned off turn back on. The TV turns on by itself.

Maybe George is a stubborn little ghost. He wants things his way. Or maybe he is like a little kid who just wants attention. People who work at the inn don't even bother to investigate, especially if he's on the second or third floor. They just go to the bottom of the stairs and yell, as the inn-keeper did when he set a chair on the balcony to rocking, "George, stop that!" Sometimes he does.

More mischief happens at night, which isn't surprising. What kid ever wanted to go to bed at night? Maybe this spirit doesn't need to sleep and wants someone to stay awake with him. Sometimes George shakes the bed to wake up sleeping guests, but there's nothing to see when they do wake up. The staff's usual response is, "Oh that's just George." One guest thought her bed's shaking was caused by an earthquake, but the innkeeper said that couldn't have been because the chandelier hanging above the bed never even swayed, nor had the weather service reported any seismic activity. Usually, it's all kind of fun for guests, experiencing a young boy's high spirits without actually seeing him.

The story has a dark side, though. Sometimes people hear the sound of a bullwhip cracking. A couple who stayed at the 1837 Bed and Breakfast for Thanksgiving in 1997 recorded a worrisome experience in the inn's guestbook. After a night's sound sleep following a big meal, they awoke to the sound of a cracking whip when it was barely light out. As they turned on a bedside lamp, they both noticed the smell of hay and, looking for its source, saw indentations that appeared to have been made by two small feet at the foot of the bed. Then they felt the bed bounce, as though a small person had been standing on it and jumped off. What kid hasn't loved bouncing off beds?

The couple could have just smiled at the notion of a stable hand's spirit jumping on their bed as he might have jumped in the stable hay—if it hadn't been for the terrible sound of that whip. Let's hope it was just a residual memory, a sound the spirit of young George remembered hearing from his work around the stables.

Chapter 3
Spooked Managers

The sister inns, Meeting Street Inn and Jasmine House, both created by the Limehouse family, differ in many ways. Jasmine House is a small, intimate hostelry of just eleven units, while Meeting Street Inn has fifty-six rooms. Both inns are renovated historic buildings. In the beginning, the history and contemporary comfort were the main talking points about both places, but the spooks have been sneaking in, and nobody is denying it.

Meeting Street Inn
173 Meeting Street

"We have ghosts," Allen Johnson, general manager at Meeting Street Inn, said almost nonchalantly. "Strange things do happen. Recurring things." As Allen tells it, "Every once in a while, I get a call from housekeeping about a locked room that is supposed to be empty. The housekeepers can't get in with their key to clean it. They say that something is wrong in that room." In addition to the lock that can be opened from outside the room with a guest or housekeeper key, each room at the inn has a dead bolt that can be locked from the inside and cannot be opened from the outside with guests' or housekeepers' keys. It's a safety and privacy measure for guests when they are in the room. The only key to open the dead bolt is kept locked in the inn's safe for emergencies.

When the housekeepers find the door locked, their first concern is that someone is inside, ill or worse. It gets worrisome because they know the guests are supposed to have checked out. Allen, or whoever is on duty, retrieves the key from the safe, knocks several times on the room door, and when no one answers, opens the dead bolt. The room is always empty, and there seems to be no way the dead bolt could have been locked. This strange event happens "periodically," according to Allen, but not in any predictable pattern.

It's not a new phenomenon at Meeting Street Inn. Reports of similar incidents date back to at least 2000. The original building was a two-story brick structure, and from time to time people involved in the various enterprises it housed lived on the second floor. Over the years this building underwent many renovations. Today it comprises fifty-six rooms, with piazzas overlooking a courtyard. But before it was renovated as a luxury hotel, the place saw many occupants and changing fortunes. It opened as Charleston Theater in 1837 and was ruined by fire in 1861. After that, with much rebuilding and remodeling, the building served variously as a saloon and restaurant, the business site for a wholesaler of German beer and Rhine wine, a brewing and ice company, a boutique, an auto parts shop, and a dental supply facility.

The building was renovated and expanded as Meeting Street Inn in 1981, gradually went downhill, and was dealt a near-knockout blow by Hurricane Hugo in 1989. Franki Limehouse, who has been a leading influence in renovating Charleston's old buildings, was the force behind the renovation that created today's luxury hotel. During the decades when the Meeting Street Inn building alternately flourished and failed, the second floor sometimes served as living quarters for people running the businesses.

Brien Limehouse, whose family owns several inns in Charleston, including the Meeting House Inn, shared one unnerving experience with Sheila Turnage when she was collecting stories for *Haunted Inns of the Southeast*. Turnage's intention was to provide brief accounts of the supernatural events in each inn along with details about staying there for people hoping to have a paranormal experience.

In Brien's experience, room 303 might be a good pick. He told Sheila that he left work late one night, instructing the night manager to call him if any problems arose—all strictly routine. Just a few minutes after midnight, he got a call. The guest in room 303 couldn't get into his room. Even with his key, he could not budge the door.

Brien had already put in a long day, not leaving work until 11:00 p.m., but he hustled back to Meeting Street Inn right away, where he found his night manager and the guest. They said the door was locked, and neither the guest nor the manager had been able to open it. That surely meant somebody had locked himself inside using the dead bolt, probably for laughs or perhaps out of spite for some personal reason.

Trying not to sigh out loud, Brien went downstairs for the master key to the safe. As soon as he got back, he tried it on the door's dead bolt. The bolt slid open easily on the first try. Brien started to open the door, relieved as it started to swing in by a fraction of an inch. Abruptly, the smooth opening motion stopped, and something inside the room slammed the door shut and held it there. Figuring whoever was inside was a big guy that several people together could outweigh, Brien, the night manager, and the guest all pushed at once. The door flew open as if there had never been any resistance from inside, leaving everybody off balance and feeling a little silly for having been tricked.

The obvious next step was to find whoever had been flexing big muscle inside the room. The group looked everywhere—under the bed, in the bathroom, behind the shower curtain, inside the closet. They didn't find anyone. Even in spacious inns, guest rooms don't have many hiding spots, and when there were no more places to look, Brien invited the guest to move to a different room. Surprisingly, the guest wasn't all that bothered and chose to stay in room 303. Nothing else unusual happened that night. Even though the guest wasn't upset about the incident, Brien was. He knew such things were not supposed to happen.

He was even more dismayed sometime later when he got another nighttime call, this one from guests in room 307 claiming that a female ghost had materialized in their room. She was gone now. "She just walked out," the guests said. Brien must have been thinking, "Is this a joke? Am I on *Candid Camera*?" Are these people bored and looking for amusement at the inn's expense?

But he went to room 307 right away, where he found the door open and the couple sitting on the bed looking bewildered. They could hardly have faked their confusion. They told Brien that the top half of a woman's body had materialized at the foot of their bed, while the bottom half just wasn't there. It's not uncommon for people in Charleston to report specters missing some part of their body, but the idea that this ghost materialized through a wall, then opened a door to leave when she didn't have legs, went beyond most ghostly episodes.

Brien speculated that this might have been the spirit of a family member of one the building's previous owners who lived upstairs. Whatever is going on, Allen Johnson's comment is an understated, "It's kind of freaky." Brien speculates that some of the spirits that still hang around may have lived somewhere in the building in the past and are trying to grasp what their "home" has become after so many renovations.

His experience at Jasmine House is harder to explain.

Jasmine House
64 Hassell Street

Only one apparition has been reported at the Jasmine House so far, but she was a bad-tempered one.

Brien Limehouse, also the general manager of Jasmine House, had no notion that this bed-and-breakfast was haunted until the morning he got a phone call from one of the guests, a traveling businessman. The guest complained that a spooky old woman, some kind of phantom, had him cornered in his room so he could not get out. People who work in the hospitality business hear all kinds of complaints, but nobody at Jasmine House had heard anything like this. In fact, guests usually commented on the charm of the rooms with their fourteen-foot-high ceilings and the pleasure of sweet tea or wine and snacks on the veranda in the afternoon. They report on the attractive decor and friendly staff here, and many plan to return each time they're in Charleston. But spooks? Some places, including Meeting Street Inn, have them (or say they do to attract adventurous guests). But not Jasmine House.

Then one businessman changed all that. Businessmen who travel a lot get good at settling into their accommodations, doing a little work, and moving on the next morning. One man who traveled this way for many years said he often had to check his newspaper to remember where he was. But the man who encountered a mean female apparition in the Chrysanthemum Room at Jasmine House won't forget where he was that morning, and he probably won't be back.

Ordinarily, the Jasmine House is a low-key hostelry, just six rooms in the 1845 Greek Revival mansion, a third-floor walk-up suite, and four more in what is now called the carriage house. The carriage house structure was originally the kitchen, detached from the main house so that if something caught fire on the stove, both buildings would not burn. There are no reports of such a crisis happening. In fact, as far as anyone knows, the place has no dark secrets and nothing to suggest haunting ever went on here. It should have been an ideal stopping place for a traveling businessman, and he went to bed believing that it was.

But when he woke up in the morning, he was confronted by the apparition of an angry woman. She didn't speak, but she made it clear that she didn't want the man to leave. She hovered, trapping him in one corner of the room and scaring him in the process. He made it to the phone to call the front desk. Then, when he closed up his suitcase and put away his laptop, he said that the angry spirit tore up his newspaper. She ripped the whole paper into tiny pieces and threw them around the room like confetti, then tossed his mail all over the floor. It would take an ordinary person a good bit of time to tear up an entire newspaper into confetti-size pieces by hand; there was no electric shredder around. The angry ghost seemed to do it in one huge puff, and the pieces fell to the floor like snow. It's not the kind of experience one would expect staying in a room named for a flower. The poor man must have felt a little unmanly calling the desk for help getting out of there.

Of course Brien got to the room right away and saw, in addition to the indignant businessman, evidence that something odd had indeed happened there, leaving paper scattered all over the floor. The angry ghost had not stayed around to meet Brien, though, so nobody was trapped in the room any longer. The businessman just wanted to leave. He asked Brien to let the staff know that it was not he who had made this mess for them to clean up. He gathered his business papers, packed his briefcase, and got out of there in a hurry.

Nobody has reported another ghostly experience at Jasmine House, leading some to speculate that the haunting was about the gentleman, not about the inn. Could it be that traveling ghosts prowl from place to place, looking for ways to vent their anger over old frustrations? If they do, would they float from inn to inn, looking for people to harass, or would they stick with one traveler? If the haunting is a skirmish between a traveler and the spirit, would one haunting be enough, or will that poor businessman be doomed to have the angry apparition follow him on his business trips from now on?

Or, if it's really the inn that is haunted, should the people at Jasmine House expect more scary episodes?

Chapter 4

Poor Ned Persists

Francis Marion Hotel
387 King Street

When the Francis Marion Hotel was built in 1924, it was the largest, grandest hotel in Charleston. In 1996 the hotel underwent extensive restoration. The hotel rises twelve stories high, with 226 rooms and suites. A young man from Manhattan, whose romantic plans in Charleston didn't work out, leapt or fell from a window on the tenth floor in 1930. Guests and employees at the hotel say he still wanders around the hotel. Sometimes they see him; sometimes he makes his presence known without appearing.

The people at the Francis Marion Hotel call Ned Cohen "our ghost," rather proud to be haunted by such a charming spirit. When guests report waking to find the drapes in their room blowing at an open window, the staff members just tell his story.

Ned Cohen lived in Manhattan and worked for Florsheim Shoes. He was a good-looking guy, personable, and used to meeting new people. Before the stock market crashed on October 29, 1929, marking the beginning of the Great Depression, he spent time, as did many young people, enjoying life as one great party. There was music everywhere—from gramophones to live performers at New York jazz clubs. The Charleston was a wildly popular dance. Women were moving away from the narrow, restricted lives of earlier times. Practically everybody was having fun.

That was when Ned Cohen met a lively young woman from Charleston, pretty and charming enough to be called a Southern belle. Undoubtedly she spoke in the soft Southern accent that persists in Charleston to this day, but unlike the Charleston women of earlier times, she did not feel restrained by the social rules of Southern society. When she met Ned, it might have been her first time away from home, and surely her first time in Manhattan, where everything moved fast and excitement filled the atmosphere. She could afford a vacation trip, which suggested that her Charleston family was well-to-do.

Not that her financial status mattered to Ned in the moment. They were two energetic, comely young people who were attracted to each other in a time and place that allowed them lots of freedom. They used that freedom to full advantage and took a long, romantic, three-day weekend. After the weekend was over, the young woman went home. That might have been the end of it—a great encounter in its time and place.

But Ned was smitten. Goodness knows he was neither the first nor the last person to be utterly charmed by a Southern belle with a melodious accent. He even talked about it a bit with his friends and some of his coworkers. They could see that he wasn't going to be content until he was able to see the girl again, so they were not surprised when he asked Florsheim Shoes to send him to Charleston. The company booked him a room at the Francis Marion Hotel in Marion Square. The square was an up-and-coming area where ladies went to shop for trendy clothes—and shoes, of course, so the location made sense to Ned. This business trip was probably for a specific project, not a permanent transfer, but that did not matter. Ned set about finding his girl there and was surely looking forward to another weekend as romantic as the first.

It didn't work out. Nobody can say exactly what went on; the pair may have spent at least an afternoon or night together, maybe even most of the weekend. But they had no fond farewell. Maybe Ned fell asleep and woke to find this unsigned note: "I am sorry. My family will never understand us. Goodby."

The next thing anybody knew, Ned was splattered in the middle of King Street. He had jumped or fallen from a room high in the building where he had been staying, which may explain why his ghostly presence often hangs around the tenth floor. In his room, authorities found Ned's suit jacket hanging in the closet, with the farewell note in the pocket. The window was wide open, and the silken drapes were blowing in the wind. Nobody could say whether Ned had jumped deliberately or perhaps had fallen after soothing his broken heart with too many drinks, but obviously, however it happened, he had gone out that window. Investigators did not take seriously the possibility that he had been pushed at the time, well before the era of sophisticated forensic testing.

One woman who stayed in one of the rooms below Ned's had an experience that suggested how Ned might have felt, realizing the finality of the moment, as he fell. It was in the year 2011, long after Ned's time. She and her husband liked their room, but not the bathroom. It was small—very small. Bathrooms did not have pride of place in a hotel (or in a home) in the 1920s, when the Francis Marion was built, and enlarging them in historic buildings is difficult. In many of the rooms at the hotel today, the bathroom is large enough to accommodate basic fixtures but not much more.

The woman and her husband planned to check out the next day to find something a little more modern. In the meantime, she was applying her makeup in a mirror outside the bathroom on the side of a cupboard. In the process, she caught the reflection of a room window. Though she was focused mainly on getting her face on right, she thought she saw a fleeting shadow pass outside the window, moving from above to below. *My imagination?* she wondered. Then, shortly afterward, she saw the shadow reflected again, as though falling from above the window, and this time she was certain she had not imagined anything. Shortly after that, the bellman brought the rest of the couple's bags to the room. "Have you seen our ghost yet?" he asked.

"Ah, he jumped, didn't he?" she said. She must have been one of those people who are attuned to otherworldly possibilities when they experience something uncommon. After learning the story of Ned, she and her husband decided to stay in this room, despite the tiny bath, because they felt connected with a piece of history. In paranormal language, what she saw could have been a residual haunting, an instance of a spirit remaining locked in a single moment that repeats over and over. That would explain why the guest saw Ned's fall reflected in the mirror repeatedly, even though in life he could have fallen only once.

In this case, though, if that is what is happening to Ned, he isn't confined just to the moment when he fell from the window. He manifests in other ways, reflecting other moods.

Sometimes Ned's presence seems to be demanding attention, one more chance to make his case. Guests in room 1010 who came in to find the TV turned on at ear-splitting volume thought so. They had not watched television at all. Turning it on and then playing it uncommonly loud seemed like a way to get someone to listen. So did stopping an elevator one floor away from the one a couple had signaled for their floor, as if Ned wanted a chance to say, "Just let me tell you my side of the story."

Could the spirit have been throwing a tantrum, angry at the girl who left him and the sorry turn his life took? Why else would he move guests' belongings to places different from where they had been left?

Or might it be that he was sadly missing his love and their special weekends together? That would explain the times a guest has been wakened by a silent, light brush on the cheek and nothing more. Of course, such a sensation could also be the result of a false awakening, a phenomenon where a person is actually dreaming when she believes herself to be awake.

Other guests have reported waking up to the sound of a window in the room going up and to the sight of the drapes blowing in the wind. They say the curtains seem to be reaching toward them. When you are jerked out of sleep, curtains flapping might look distressingly like ghostly movement, even if you had not heard the hotel staff boast about Ned's presence.

Today, guest room decor in the hotel reflects the Roaring Twenties era, when life was easy and fun, when Ned Cohen met a Southern belle in Manhattan. Maybe he hangs around the upper rooms these days because it is all so familiar and reminds him of his short romance. When people in the hotel actually see Ned, he is still in shirtsleeves. After all, his jacket was in the closet when he died. They say he appears wandering in the halls, confused, as if still puzzling over why he lost his girl. He was in a good position as a favored employee with Florsheim Shoes, after all, and probably could have been transferred to Charleston to manage an upscale shop in Marion Square. He would have earned a good salary and his position would have been respectable, so why shouldn't her family understand them?

But Ned was a Yankee with a Jewish name. He could not have known that to her Southern family, which may well have remained financially secure despite the Great Depression, he would never enjoy the same social status as she. To them, no matter what job title he held, he would always be a shoe salesman, and no shoe salesman would be regarded well by the elite. His girl may have been up for a fling, a fun vacation in the Big City, and another romantic encounter in Charleston's finest hotel, but perhaps she felt that in continuing a relationship with him, she had too much to lose.

Whatever happened, the haunting stories vary enough in detail to make a single explanation of the haunting insufficient. Maybe Ned's ghostly behavior is similar to the experience we all have sometimes, of *remembering* a particular unpleasant event over and over, even as we go about other activities.

As for the people at the Marion Hotel, Ned Cohen is *their* ghost and they welcome him. After participating in ghost tours around the city booked by the hotel, guests receive a leaflet that tells Ned's story. The hotel's enthusiasm in promoting Ned's presence provides a degree of respectability he could not have hoped to achieve as a Yankee courting a Southern belle in 1920s Charleston. Maybe his persistence is rewarded now. That might be reason enough for him to keep hanging around.

Chapter 5

The Half-Head Cadet

Embassy Suites
337 Meeting Street

The Embassy Suites hotel is housed in a building dating back to 1829. The building served various military purposes before opening in 1843 as the South Carolina Military College, known today as the Citadel. A history of violence once plagued the school, especially suicides and hazing of new cadets who were not white. After the Citadel moved to its current location on the Ashley River in 1992, the old building was restored and renovated to become the Embassy Suites. Hotel staff encountered so many ghosts connected to the property's grim history that the workers were told not to talk to guests about them. The apparition seen most often is a young man in a gray military uniform who looks perfectly normal, except that the top of his head is missing.

Unlike some of Charleston's haunted inns, Embassy Suites does not publicize the paranormal experiences guests and staff have experienced in the building, although hotel staff are free to talk about them now. In 2004 three members of the Paranormal Research Society of North America (PRSNA) studied activities at the hotel for three days, with the cooperation of the management. In her written report, society founder Hillary Murdoch thanked the staff and managers for their warm reception. The team had wanted to stay in mezzanine room M113, where "Half Head" shows up most often. Guests aren't assigned to the room unless the rest of the house is full. Unfortunately, it turned out to be one of the few rooms in which smoking is permitted, so after catching a whiff, the team chose instead to sleep in rooms 105 and 231, where guests have reported seeing other ghosts.

The stories about Half Head, however, are the most unnerving. One of the best known is told by Ed Macy and Geordie Buxton in *Haunted Charleston*. Belgian heart surgeon Dr. Anna Fletcher, a guest in the hotel, had an experience one night in September 2003 that threatened to stop her own heart. It was about 3:00 a.m., an hour when sleep researchers say most of us are especially relaxed, because at some subconscious level we feel the most dangerous part of the night has passed safely. But something woke Dr. Fletcher, and, like a true medical professional, she sprang from deep sleep to activity in an instant.

She saw the figure of a young man in a gray military uniform standing between her bed and the door. She saw right away that the top of his head was missing. It was not bleeding or messy, just gone. She said the cadet looked confused, as though he did not know where he was or why. In a heartbeat, Dr. Fletcher was out of bed, scantily clad (to put it mildly), headed for the door in a collision course with the young man. Running like that, she expected to knock him down, but he wasn't solid. She raced right on through his ghostly form and down the stairs, where someone on staff quickly got her into a robe and arranged a ride for her to the neighboring Francis Marion Hotel. She spent the rest of the night there, wide awake. Of course the Francis Marion also has its ghostly male, Ned, who hangs around the hotel, but nobody mentioned that to her and nothing unusual happened to her there, which was a blessing. In a telephone conversation with Macy and Buxton months later, the surgeon said she still could not grasp what had happened that night, but the experience was absolutely real.

Dr. Fletcher had no idea that earlier, in 2002, Half Head had been the topic of ongoing Internet blog discussions. It started after a man on his honeymoon wrote an essay, "Praising Charleston," on PhotoDude.com. The honeymooners had taken a ghost tour that, to their surprise, ended at their own hotel, the Embassy Suites. The husband repeated the Half Head story as it had been told on the tour, adding that neither he nor his wife had seen anything unusual.

Responses from people who read that comment got right to the spooky point: Half Head was real and the hotel was haunted. One person wrote, "I work at Embassy Suites in the maintenance department and I can tell you that 'Half Head' is as prominent now as in the past. He regularly shows up in our housekeeping areas and service elevator and sometimes rattles our supply lockers on the 4th floor housekeeping area." The maintenance worker's account said the apparition had been reported at the end of August 2000, on the bed of a sleeping woman who woke feeling she was not alone. Rather than scuttle for the door, she asked who was there. The spirit said his name was George, and he was looking for his lost pocketknife. Was she very brave or very curious? She reached around to touch the source of the voice and found that his head "was not all there." After that, her courage must have run out, because next morning she asked to be moved to another room. The maintenance worker said that an old pocketknife is part of a display in the lobby of artifacts excavated on the property.

In a further exchange of posts on August 30, 2003, Geri Griffin wrote that she and her sister had booked a room at the Embassy Suites for three nights that August because they thought they would enjoy the history of the old building. Apparently the sisters experienced a lot more than just history. Geri woke in the middle of the first night feeling pressure, as if someone were pressing on her neck. She shook it off.

In the morning her sister said that someone had tried to get into her bed too. When he bent down so she could see him, she noticed blond hair and—yep—half a head. "I'm not very pretty," he told her. He also told her his name, but in the morning she could not remember it, though she did remember that he said to tell "them" he was looking for his pocketknife. The sisters had further experiences with the presence the next night, but they did not feel threatened—just crowded in their beds. Still, they paid their bill later that second day so that if anything more happened on the third night, they could get out fast without defaulting.

The people at the front desk told the sisters they had met the hotel ghost. (Charleston is so full of ghosts that you can say things like that and nobody looks askance.) Later, the housekeeping manager came to the sisters' room to chat, explaining that employees were not supposed to talk to guests about the hotel's ghosts. She did it anyway. She said the experiences of her crew included cupboards opening and closing, objects flying at them as if thrown, utility carts moving by themselves, and seeing groups of ghosts in Citadel uniforms clustered in the main hall. She assured the sisters that Half Head was harmless. Most guests just let him sleep with them.

Really?

The women stuck it out for their third night, not sleeping very well, sensing a presence in their beds but not sure whether they were encountering Half Head again or dreaming.

The maintenance worker had written in the blog, "I think it only fair to say that we probably can't blame 'halfhead' [*sic*] for everything we witness here because I'm sure there are more ghosts (spirits, if you will) hanging around."

Generations of violence on the property may have created generations of ghosts. The only thing there before 1822 was a small state tobacco inspection station, but that changed when city leaders heard that a slave rebellion plot was in the works. They accused Denmark Vesey, a free black man, of organizing the revolt, and in short order the city hanged Vesey and his alleged conspirators. For security, South Carolina built a fortress where the tobacco station had once stood, and state troops manned the site from 1832 until 1843, when the Citadel opened as the Military College of South Carolina. Traditionally, some parents have considered military schools a good way to manage difficult sons. The sons did not always agree. Some chose suicide. Others tormented new cadets. The school became notorious for episodes of hazing, especially of black cadets and, later, of the first women to be admitted. Perhaps some of the cadets who killed themselves never quite got away. And while nobody has identified a ghost as female, who better than an early female victim of hazing to know exactly how to aggravate the housekeepers of Embassy Suites? Some guests have reported seeing men in Civil War uniforms at the fountain in the atrium before dawn. Typically guests have assumed it was a gathering of Civil War reenactors, but come daylight they would learn that no Confederate reenactors had been in the hotel. Could these apparitions date back to the days when the state troops kept order at the site?

The sister guests left Embassy Suites convinced by their experiences with Half Head that ghosts really do exist. Geri wrote, "They should give him back the damn penknife!"

The PRSNA team did not have such dramatic experiences, but their cameras, digital voice recorder, and other equipment did record some unusual occurrences. They took anomalous photos in room M113, pictures that did not seem to belong in that scene, although their report didn't describe them. The team experimented with moving a few small items in Half Head's room. Later they found them returned to their original places. But the first rule of good paranormal investigators is to assume supernatural causes only after they have ruled out all other possibilities. The team decided a housekeeper might have been in the room and put things back where she thought they belonged.

The investigators also got a picture of a pink orb in M113 and, by the end of their stay, had collected other anomalous photos. Their equipment recorded spikes in electromagnetic fields, an occurrence often associated with haunting. They concluded that their findings, while not dramatic, indicated a significant level of unexplained activity. PRSNA urges other investigators to check out the Embassy Suites and share their findings.

Meanwhile, Half Head still hangs around some of the guest rooms. These days, though, it is okay for the staff to talk about it, and management now welcomes paranormal investigators. As an experiment, investigators might try taking the old pocketknife out of the lobby display and putting it in room M113. If he got his knife back, would Half Head go away for good?

Chapter 6

An Old Woman
and a Pooch

Poogan's Porch
72 Queen Street

The Victorian house was already one hundred years old when Bob-
bie Ball bought it and began renovating it to become Poogan's
Porch restaurant. It opened in 1976. Bobbie, restaurant staff,
patrons, and outside observers have had experiences, often involv-
ing an old woman in a long black dress, that they say can be
explained only by the supernatural. Some people see a friendly dog
wagging his tail in the yard too. They think it's Poogan, who died in
1979 and is buried there.

George and Emily were strolling around the Mills House Hotel,
which fronts on Meeting Street and faces Queen Street on
one side, just across from Poogan's Porch restaurant. It was
late. The restaurant was closed and dark, but Emily heard
a noise then saw movement at one of the windows—an old
woman who seemed to be pounding to be let out. Emily
thought maybe the poor woman had been locked inside by
accident and suggested to George that they call the local
police to let her out.

A little shaken, George and Emily told their story to a
desk clerk when they went back inside the hotel, which they
did rather quickly. The clerk didn't laugh at them as they'd
expected. "Oh, yes," she said. "Guests do see a ghost at

Poogan's Porch from time to time. We think it must be Zoe, who once lived in the house. Sometimes guests specifically ask to book second-floor rooms on that side of the hotel so they can watch for her." When the police arrived, nothing seemed disturbed. The restaurant was empty. The door was still locked, the alarm still set, and nothing inside seemed changed. The officers were not surprised, because they had responded to similar nighttime calls in the past.

Poogan's Porch is a busy, popular place, named for a neighborhood dog that hung around the porch, accepting handouts and petting from diners. Some people come to eat here because it's known for traditional Lowcountry cuisine that is ramped up a notch with a touch of gourmet influence and great wines. One employee says the shrimp and grits are "arguably the best in the South." Nobody has been known to criticize the biscuits with honey butter, either. One guest who had reservations about some of what she ate, nevertheless said, "The biscuits were flipping amazing."

Other guests come hoping to glimpse a ghost along with their grits, especially since the Travel Channel named Poogan's Porch one of the most haunted restaurants in the world. How they decided that is as much a mystery as the haunting spirits, some travelers say.

Certainly this isn't a place that needs ghostly publicity. Bobbie Ball; her husband, Chuck; and their son, Brad, are managing partners in the business. Brad worked his way from the ground up, starting as a delivery boy for the restaurant, attending an intensive culinary arts program in New York City, and becoming a certified sommelier. Their experienced executive chef adds what has been called "a gourmet spin on Southern food" to the classic Lowcountry specialties. The restaurant participates in South Carolina's "farm-to-fork" program, emphasizing locally, sustainably produced seafood, meats, and produce. The indoor restaurant seating is intimate, in several smaller rooms rather than in a single, large clattering dining hall. And the porch is considered the dining area of choice in good weather, even without Poogan.

But ghost stories are part of the restaurant's lore, even if they're not needed to attract guests. Strange things keep happening, and it's better to capitalize on them than try to deny them.

Here's an example involving people who came only to eat, never having heard about a ghost. A young couple wanted to celebrate their recent engagement. After they'd ordered, the young woman excused herself to go to the ladies' room. Minutes later, she heard the doorknob rattling and then someone knocking at the door. "I'll be out in just a minute," she called, thinking, not for the first time, how unfair it was that men could do these things so much more quickly than women. The knocking and rattling continued, louder than ever. "I said just a minute, please," she said, a little more forcefully. That kind of impatience was just plain rude.

While she was washing her hands, the noise stopped abruptly. "That's better," she muttered under her breath. But then as she looked up to reach for a towel, she was shocked to see an old woman in the mirror behind her. The woman was dressed in a long black dress and a worn-looking sweater. With a shriek, the bride-to-be burst out of the ladies' room, hands still wet, and ran past the table where her fiancé sat waiting. She tore out the front door, down the porch steps, and into the yard, crying hysterically. Even though a staff member checked the ladies' room and assured her it was empty, the young woman refused to go back into the restaurant, not even for she-crab soup and a complimentary meal. Not then, not ever.

Other people's experiences have been less traumatic. Some folks even find their sightings sweetly sad. According to local lore, the ghost is probably Zoe Saint Armand. She and her sister, Elizabeth, both unmarried schoolteachers, lived in the house at 72 Queen Street that is now Poogan's Porch. As a teacher, Zoe was known to be strict, expecting her students to put their full effort into their studies. Aside from school, the sisters kept to themselves, socializing with others only rarely, a cat their only companion.

Elizabeth died in 1945. Later, their cat died too. Zoe was no longer teaching, and without that occupation or her two companions, she got lonely. Sometimes she stood on the second-floor balcony and waved to people passing by, perhaps inviting them to stop in for a chat.

Passers-by these days who see her as a waving ghost believe she is still inviting them to visit. One tourist, who snapped a picture of a pale face behind the lace curtain at an upstairs window, was sure the poor thing just wanted company, but her companion hustled her away, muttering, "Don't even think about it." Later, looking at the photo, the tourist wasn't so sure about the face. She had heard about something known as "matrixing," or the tendency of the human brain to find significant patterns in abstract designs. To her it still looked like a face behind that curtain, but she wasn't willing to argue about it.

Guests and staff inside the restaurant have had much different experiences, more suggestive of anger and impatience than of loneliness. That reflects Zoe's strict and demanding side, what you might expect from a teacher who was a strong disciplinarian and isn't pleased about what has happened to the rooms that used to be her home. Bobbie claims that once, when she was closing up for the night, wooden doors in the house slammed open. The doors were too heavy to have been affected by wind, especially since the outside doors and windows were all closed. At the same time, large wooden stools in the kitchen fell over. Did Zoe disapprove of something in Bobbie's routine? Or was she objecting to having her home turned into a public eating place?

At least one chef thinks so. He came in one morning to begin the day's preparations, poured himself a cup of coffee, then left it on the counter while he went to open the back door for a food vendor. When he got back to the kitchen, his mug was empty, though he hadn't had a minute to drink any coffee. Thinking he hadn't even had time to pour it, he picked up the mug and reached for the coffee pot. Then he discovered traces of lipstick on the rim of the mug. What would a ghost do with coffee? Did Zoe wear lipstick? Could there have been a brief glitch with the dishwasher that left the mug not quite clean? Or was Zoe again expressing her displeasure at her home being a restaurant?

One waiter thinks she was. He had gone to check a second-floor dining room to make sure it was ready for the next day. At first everything looked normal—crisp, clean tablecloths in place and chairs pulled away from the tables so that they would not push against the cloths and wrinkle them. Then the waiter noticed that at one table, a chair was pulled close, pushing the cloth underneath, as though a person were sitting there. Nothing happened as he pulled the chair out, but telling the story still makes him uneasy. He was sure nobody had been up there since the room had been cleaned up earlier that night.

A number of people have said that while they never saw anything unusual, they did feel unwelcome, with a sense that something bad might happen. One woman took pictures of two orbs around the porch and roof of the house. She wonders if they could be the spirits of Zoe and her sister, still wishing intruders would go away.

If Zoe resents restaurant customers and help, she must get into fits about the ghost tours that come into the restaurant. A waitress tells the story of a tour guide bringing in a group at lunchtime, not to eat but to hear Zoe's story. But the story the waitress heard bore no resemblance to the known facts. The guide pointed to a staircase and said, "This is where Zoe fell down the steps and broke her neck." That simply did not happen. It would not be unreasonable for her to be angry enough about such misinformation to devise ways to keep people from coming back to the restaurant. (It is worth mentioning that many guides learn the most likely and best documented stories to tell. They may tell them with a flourish, but they would not make things up.)

But a morning chef had an experience he thinks demonstrates Zoe's compassion. He was always on time, getting to the kitchen early in the morning to begin preparations for the day's menu. He liked his job and took it seriously. One night he set his alarm carefully as usual and went to sleep. The next morning he woke long after he should have been at work and saw that his alarm clock hadn't gone off because it was broken. That clock had been fine the night before; he was sure of it.

When he finally got to work, fully prepared to apologize profusely, he learned that there had been a serious early-morning fire in the kitchen, and to this day he believes that Zoe saved his life by manipulating his clock so that he would still be safely home in bed when the fire raged.

But let's not forget Poogan, the pooch for whom the restaurant was named. He died in 1979. His grave is marked with a headstone and a little statue of him looking sweet and friendly. Yet some guests insist that as they leave the restaurant, they see a little dog wagging his tail there in the yard. Little kids see the dog more often than adults. You would expect that, as young'uns typically beg for a puppy that their parents may or may not want. From a kid's point of view, if they can "see" Poogan, maybe that will be enough to persuade Mom and Dad that they really deserve a dog.

As for why he would hang around, it makes sense, in a way. If you'd had a great time being the Poogan's Porch pooch, with your own special spot, getting affection and tasty tidbits from diners, wouldn't you want to come back from time to time to the place where everybody petted and pampered you?

Chapter 7
Spirits and a Spirit

Southend Brewery
161 East Bay Street

The proprietors of Southend Brewery and Smokehouse claim their old building, looking over the Charleston Harbor, is one of the most haunted in the city. A cotton merchant who was down on his luck hanged himself inside when he saw his ship, loaded with the cotton that he hoped would get him out of debt, destroyed by fire. His suicide became highly publicized after his blood dripped through the floor to the sidewalk below, attracting birds that pecked at his face. People still see him in the building, where unexplained things happen—but, oddly, he seems happy now.

Sally and Adam Ressa spent a weekend in Charleston to celebrate their wedding anniversary. Unlike many visitors, they did not go on a ghost tour. Adam insisted that there was no such thing as ghosts, but Sally had had a spooky experience in the bathroom at Poogan's Porch (see page 34) when she was ten years old that scared her so much that she usually avoids places where ghosts are even a possibility. So they sure didn't go to the Southend Brewery on a ghost hunt; they went because Adam was a home brewer, and he wanted to sample their craft beers. Sally agreed because she was a good wife who wanted Adam to be happy. They did ask their waiter about the resident spirit, but he didn't have much to say except that somebody had hanged himself on the third floor a long time ago.

That somebody was George Poirier. And the three-story building, long before it became a brewery, was built by F. W. Wagener in 1880 to serve as warehouse, office, and retail space for his business, F. W. Wagener and Company. The first-floor retail facility sold everything from marine supplies to liquor and food. It was the kind of store where people might stock up before taking to sea, and, located so close to the water, it did well financially. But the cotton and the phosphate fertilizer that Wagener shipped from his warehouse were the big moneymakers.

Poirier and his family, antebellum planters and merchants and F. W. Wagener clients, had made a lot of money without ever having to work very hard. Although the Civil War left many once well-to-do Charlestonians destitute, as Ed Macy and Julian T. Buxton III tell the history in *The Ghosts of Charleston,* the Poirier family, recognizing the danger to their wealth, had quietly invested in businesses in England and in United States bonds. So after the Civil War, George Poirier was still well off, inheriting a profitable, working plantation. The trouble was, he didn't know how to run it, nor could he manage his financial affairs sensibly. Soon his field hands were leaving, his money was gone, he was in debt, and he was operating on the hope that the one load of cotton he'd managed to broker through Wagener would earn enough money to invest in new directions and turn his fortunes around.

The cotton was on a ship set to sail late in the evening, and Poirier was at a window overlooking the harbor, watching the ship that carried his last chance at economic recovery. He was hopeful. He could almost imagine buying fine new clothes and living graciously once again as he watched the slow progress of the ship.

Then he saw something strange. He squinted and tried to focus on what he was seeing. Smoke! Smoke was rising from the ship, slowly at first, then getting thicker until flames burst through. George Poirier watched from the warehouse office, which had tall windows on two sides, as his last hope burned in the water until there was no possible chance of salvaging anything. The fire may have started because a sailor who'd drunk too much from the Wagener store's rum stock dropped his pipe, setting bales of cotton on fire.

It didn't really matter to George what started it; he knew he was finished. He found a length of the same rope used for securing the cotton bales and made a noose that he hung around his neck. Then he stood on a chair balanced atop a table, flipped the rope over a high beam, tied it, and kicked the chair out from under himself.

Some might say it was a permanent solution to a temporary problem. Either way, why the fuss over his death? In bad times, other men have hanged themselves and the event has faded quietly into the past. Perhaps that would've been Poirier's fate too, had not large falcons seen his dangling body as the sunlight hit the long windows. They burst in from under the eaves, more and more of them, pecking at the dead man's face until his blood dripped down to the floors and sidewalk below. In an even gorier version of the story, Poirier used baling wire to hang himself, the motion of his body plunged the chair through the window, and the wire noose cut off his head. Blood drenched the floor and dripped to the floors below, while the chair and broken window glass littered the sidewalk outside, and seagulls flew away from the building with pieces of human flesh in their beaks.

Maybe the memory of the awful event was too strong in the minds of people who saw it, or maybe Poirier changed his mind when it was too late. For whatever reason, his spirit hangs around the three-story building at 161 East Bay Street, behaving unpleasantly. People sometimes think they see the angry movements of a specter inside as they walk past the building. Some have even changed their walking routes around the battery to avoid passing the building at all.

By 1983 the place had become the East Bay Trading Company Restaurant, a popular place for locals and tourists alike. Nothing much happened during business hours, but at the end of one day, when the restaurant's employees and a few from other restaurants gathered for a bit of beer and chatter, the atmosphere changed. Because the sun beat through the windows all day, the upstairs room was sometimes hot enough to make you sweat, bearable only thanks to air-conditioning. But on this hot summer night, the group sitting around the tables in the room heard an uncanny sound, like wind blowing through the windows—except the windows were shut. The temperature dropped. (Sudden drops in temperature are often associated with hauntings.) The wind blew harder, reaching hurricane strength. The employees wondered how wind could blow through closed windows. At the same time, an odd light winked for a moment in the rafters high above. Nobody knew what to make of it, except that it was an unnatural occurrence.

Even after that scary experience, the staff still gathered on the third floor to unwind at the end of the workday. After all, this was Charleston. Odd things often happened. When the cold wind blew in again, they were disconcerted, but they might have discounted even that had they not found a pile of heavy furniture heaped into a huge mess on the third floor. At the top of the pile, a chair that looked like the one Poirier used to reach the rafters with his noose rocked slowly, no longer a broken mass of splinters. That didn't last long, though. The chair flew off the top of the pile like a projectile, hitting the floor and falling to pieces at the feet of the restaurant owner.

The building now houses a restaurant, Southend Brewing Company and Smokehouse, which opened in 1997. It operates as a brewpub, restaurant, and bar, with a dance floor. Although the place has been remodeled, the center of the space, from the first to third floors, remains open, as it was in the past. One visitor was awed by the fact that she could see all the way from the first floor up to the roof in this space. She remarked on its "old warehousey feel." One distinctly modern feature, a glass elevator, runs from the first to the third floor. Recalling the era when employees hung around up there after work, the space is devoted now to a bar, billiards, and games, as well as bathrooms. The second floor is for catering special parties, reunions, and receptions. Both floors have a sensational view of the Charleston Harbor.

Nobody has claimed to see a shipload of cotton burning in the harbor, but guests have had experiences that suggest the old spirit still hangs around. According to the Southend Brewery website, the ghost is friendly now. He sometimes appears to guests while they are salsa dancing. Bartenders claim that sometimes beer flows from an open tap even when nobody is near it. On the third floor, servers have felt a whoosh of air at the windows overlooking the harbor, as though a tall person has gone by. Participants in special gatherings on the second floor sometimes feel as though they have an extra, uninvited guest in the party, though they don't see anyone.

Maybe Poirier decided the afterlife was too dull without the social life he'd once enjoyed as a wealthy young man. If people change, maybe ghosts can too. Some say the atmosphere of fun and relaxation at Southend Brewery has made the once miserable ghost happily sociable, so he joins in as much as he can, even if he is invisible now.

But Sally Ressa doesn't think so. When she went to the third floor to use the ladies' room, she didn't pay much attention to the play areas upstairs. She did notice, however, that a lot of tables and chairs had been stacked nearby, looking as though they had been tossed about. She got an uneasy feeling, a sense of an unfriendly presence that made her remember the experience that had scared her so badly at Poogan's Porch when she was ten. In the bathroom at Poogan's she had seen the image of an old woman "watching me pee." It was enough to scare a little girl. She had run from the bathroom sobbing. Nearly fifteen years later, going into the brewery's third-floor bathroom, she felt uneasy all over again. Something was spooking her. She couldn't blame it on alcohol, because she was pregnant and hadn't had a drop. Besides, Adam was the beer lover. But something felt wrong up there on the third floor of Southend Brewery, nothing fun like the spirit of a salsa-dancing ghost. Sally doesn't mince words: "I just wanted to get out of there," she said.

At least one other guest has reported experiences reminiscent of the old days. She said that it was so cold where she sat in the dining room that she kept her jacket on the whole time she ate. Water dripped from the ceiling onto her table, an event that the waitress didn't seem to find remarkable. It definitely was water dripping, not blood, but the old stories of George's death still come to mind.

The proprietors know the history of their place, including the grim parts, but naturally they like the idea of a happier spirit, one they call "a permanent guest." They invite guests and travelers who have felt "paranormal energy" at the brewery to tell their stories on the website blog. Maybe past visitors will report a mix of experiences. If living people can have good days and bad days, why can't a spirit?

Part Two

GRAVE HAUNTS

Tours of Charleston almost always include some of the Holy City's old churches and graveyards. In the daytime, each is a marvel of architecture and history. The tombstones mark the resting places of many famous citizens, as well as some who were infamous. After dark, ghosts have been spotted prowling the grounds, sometimes several in the same yard. But in earlier times, graveyards were peaceful places, always close to their churches, where people might take an evening stroll or quietly pay their respects to departed loved ones. As tour guides often say, where you have dead people, you have ghosts, so some of the city's enduring stories are about people who still hang around the cemeteries where they were buried. If you walk here, it is better not to do it alone—just in case.

Chapter 8
Lonely Women

St. Michael's Episcopal Churchyard
Corner of Meeting and Broad Streets

Nobody is sure about the identity of the ghost that wanders through the churchyard. It may be the spirit of a young woman who died mysteriously shortly before the wedding she'd planned in the church. Or it might be a happier ghost, a girl who was married there and just returns now to relive the moment.

St. Michael's is the oldest church building in Charleston, built in 1761 and remarkable for having kept its original design despite renovations and repairs. Its notable features include the 186-foot-high steeple and eight bells in the tower that were brought from England in 1764. George Washington worshiped here on May 8, 1791, as did Robert E. Lee about seventy years later. The church still has its original pulpit and chandelier, though the chandelier, which originally contained candles, has been electrified. In addition to its historical wonder and the active community involvement of the church members, the graveyard holds yet another kind of allure for those who love ghost stories.

One story is about seventeen-year-old Harriet Mackie, who died in 1804 just before her wedding. Although details about what happened to her are few, her story gained popularity among Charlestonians after the 1855 publication of the novel *Lily* by Susan Petigru King. The title character was based on the real-life Harriet, although the details were probably a tad distorted.

Harriet seemed to be in perfect health, happily getting ready on her wedding day. Her gown and headdress were exquisite. She truly loved the man she was about to marry. Suddenly, though, she took ill and died just a few hours later. Nobody is sure what happened, but the local legend of the time suggested that she had been poisoned.

At least one man, William Alston, might have had a motive. Harriet's father, Dr. James Mackie, a wealthy man, left a will giving everything he owned, including a large rice plantation, to Harriet—effective the day she married. But if she died before she was married, the will specified that all Dr. Mackie's holdings should go to the two sons of William Alston, a major slave owner in South Carolina. In Susan King's fictional version of the Lily/Harriet story, a sewing girl having an affair with Lily's fiancé poisoned her to prevent the wedding. In real life, William Alston, whose sons inherited Dr. Mackie's estate after Lily's death, was the more likely suspect.

After Harriet was laid out on her bed in her wedding dress to receive mourners, at least one visitor may not have mourned. Another Charleston gentleman, though, was horrified when he saw her dead body. Just six months earlier, after meeting Harriet, he had written in his diary about her "singular beauty and charm." After he saw her laid out in her wedding dress, he wrote in his diary that it was shocking how in just a few hours someone who "but yesterday seemed so lovely and so fair to view, should today appear disgusting and become the object of our aversion."

It was a custom of mourning among those who could afford it at the time to have a miniature portrait of the lost soul made. The family commissioned the artist P. R. Vallee to paint a miniature portrait of Harriet in watercolor and graphite pencil on ivory to recall and memorialize her beauty in life. The artist made her still beautiful, even in death. In the portrait she wears a rose garland to symbolize her youth and the love of her fiancé. A strand of her hair is plaited on the reverse side of the miniature as a sign of eternal love between them, and of faith that they would marry in the next life. The framed miniature measures just $3^{3}/_{16}$ x $2^{3}/_{16}$ inches and is displayed in the American Portrait and Mourning Miniatures collection at the Yale University Art Gallery.

Harriet's sad ghost is seen wandering around inside the church more often than in the graveyard. That makes sense for a young woman who still hasn't realized that she is dead and hopes the wedding will go on. Or, if it truly is the spirit of Harriet, perhaps she is waiting for her fiancé to join her to fulfill the promise of being together in the afterlife, the promise symbolized by her miniature death portrait.

In another wedding-related possibility, some folks wonder if the wandering woman might not be Maria Whaley, a fifteen-year-old girl whose father, Joseph Whaley, had enrolled her in a girls' school at 39 Legare Street, where Madame Talvande taught young women to be Charleston ladies. Colonel Joseph Whaley was trying desperately to keep young Maria away from George Morris, an older bachelor who found ways and places to meet and court her. It's not that there was anything really wrong with Morris, except that he was not from a prominent family and the colonel felt sure that Maria could make a more prestigious match. He believed learning womanly arts and manners at Madam Talvande's school would distract Maria so that she would forget all about George Morris. Doing well in this school required the girls to behave as she told them and follow her instructions exactly.

But Whaley didn't figure on the determination of a fifteen-year-old girl in love. With the help of several sympathetic friends outside the school, Maria sneaked out one night and rode in a friend's carriage to meet and marry George in St. Michael's Church. The minister, Mr. Dalcho, who had been sympathetic to the couple's wish to be together, married them in the company of a small group of friends, then gave them his blessing as they left the candlelit church. After the wedding, the plan was for Maria to return to the school by carriage and sneak back in so that, rather than leaving in a midnight elopement, she could go off properly, in the daytime, with her new husband.

But the plan started to fall apart. It was a cold and rainy night, and after an affectionate "See you in the morning, my love" in the carriage, Maria climbed out. The rain quickly drenched her demure white dress, and she was immediately wet and shivering. She slipped and fell in the mud as she got to the entrance of the school and was bedraggled and weeping when she went inside. She was lucky that the door was open, so she did not have to raise an alarm by pounding to get in. Miss Hanburn, the nighttime custodian of the girls, was so dismayed by Maria's misery that she whisked Maria away to dry clothes and a warm bed without asking how she'd come to be so wet and dirty. By morning, Maria was her usual perky self, dressed for travel but still in the manner of the other schoolgirls, so she didn't stand out.

As he'd promised, George Morris came to the school early and asked for Mrs. Morris. The school mistress, Madame Talvande, told him emphatically that no such person was there.

Maybe he was playing it cute, but George didn't explain about the night wedding; he just kept insisting that of course Mrs. Morris was there. In a fit of pique, Madame Talvande figured to get rid of him by demonstrating the absence of a Mrs. Anybody. This was a school for girls, not for married women. She called all the girls together to stand opposite George, and in a voice clearly meant to show what a stupid idea he had, said, "Is there a Mrs. Morris among you?"

"Yes, ma'am," Maria said, stepping forward with a modest smile. Of course, Madam Talvande protested that Maria's father had never mentioned her being married.

"He doesn't know," Maria said. "Mr. Morris and I were married just last night in St. Michael's church."

Madame Talvande threw what today would be called "a hissy fit," but there wasn't anything she could do. Mr. and Mrs. Morris went to their coach and drove off. Madame Talvande made up her mind that nothing like that would happen to mar her school's reputation again, so she built a high wall that was later joined by tall iron gates, called "sword gates" because of their forbidding but handsome design of spears and swords. No girl would ever again escape her school.

The property became a private home in 1849. It's not a place you can tour, but there are reports of a female ghost roaming the halls of the building. It's probably Madame Talvande, still making sure none of her girls ever escapes again, but some people think it could be Miss Hanburn, endlessly reliving the humiliation of having been outwitted by a fifteen-year-old girl.

Nobody knows how Maria's father reacted to Maria's escape, though it is said that eventually he forgave her and came to approve of George Morris. Thus, George and Maria lived happily ever after.

But if that's so, why would she be haunting the church and churchyard? Perhaps because the life of a proper, married Southern woman was not very lively in those days, with its emphasis on polite conversation, needlework, playing the piano, and singing. Not all spirits hang around where bad things have happened to them. Some return to the place they were happiest. Could it be that from time to time Maria just likes to visit the spot where her life was most exciting? Even if she and George did live happily ever after, perhaps Maria's lively spirit still craves the kind of adventure she enjoyed as a girl, defying her father and Madame Talvanade.

Chapter 9
Lovelorn Ladies

The Unitarian Church Graveyard
8 Archdale Street

Two specters have been seen prowling the Unitarian graveyard, though not together. One haunts the grave of a young woman whose father prevented her marriage to a sailor. The other wanders looking for her husband, who died far from home and was never buried in what should have been his place next to her.

Even without ghosts, the Unitarian Church Graveyard could be a scary place. Unlike most cemeteries of historical importance in Charleston, this one is not kept trimmed and clipped to tidy perfection. Wildflowers and native plants cover the ground around the tombstones, and Spanish moss drips from tree branches. The walkways are perfectly clear, though. The idea was to maintain a natural look that softens the lines of tombstones and cooperates with nature, rather than imposes unnatural order on it. The graveyard also has lots of secluded spots. Maybe that is why it has been a popular place for people to meet at night for—um—long, meaningful conversations or companionable strolls. Over the years, people have reported numerous supernatural sightings of figures no longer of this world. Each story is about love.

Probably the most popular is the story of Annabell Lee, a beautiful girl living in Charleston before the Civil War. Charlestonians like to say that Edgar Allan Poe's poem "Annabel Lee" was inspired by his brief stay in Charleston with the army in 1827, and that she is the subject of his poem. While it's true that you could think of old Charleston as a "kingdom by the sea," it's also true that Poe's wife, Virginia, had died just a couple of years before he wrote and published his poem, and she must have been on his mind when he wrote it. "Virginia by the sea" would've been a tough rhythm pattern to maintain for the length of his poem, but if Poe was still mourning Virginia's death, he could write about it using the more poetic "Annabel Lee" and "by the sea." Most students of literature agree that Poe had a tendency to write about women lost from his life and doubt he would have made too much fuss over a short meeting with a pretty girl.

But no matter—Annabell's story in Charleston is that she met a sailor who was stationed in Virginia, on duty for a while in Charleston. Sailors were well thought of in the Charlestson coastal area, and this one was bright and good-looking, with just the right personality to appeal to a lively young woman. She was as sweet as she was beautiful. Of course they fell in love, spending as much time together as they could.

Annabell's father did not like this one bit. What respectable father could approve of a relationship between a transient sailor and his daughter? He wanted her to marry someone from a good family, someone with bright prospects for wealth and social status, so he forbade her to see her sailor anymore.

But what young people in love were ever stopped by a disapproving parent? Annabell and the young man began meeting at night in a secluded spot in the Unitarian Church graveyard. This went on for several months, until Annabell's father realized she was being too cooperative—at least in the daytime—and he began to follow her surreptitiously after dark. He quickly saw that she was meeting her sailor in the cemetery. Of course he was furious.

What could he do? A gentleman wouldn't whip his daughter. In pre–Civil War Charleston, he couldn't gain control by cutting off her iPhone and Internet connection. A twenty-four-hour companion was impossible. So he locked Annabell in her room and kept her there for many months. Inevitably, the sailor was shipped back to Virginia, and the young lovers never saw one another again. Sometime later, Annabell died of scarlet fever caused by a mosquito bite.

As soon as word of Annabell's death reached the sailor, he arranged to return to Charleston so he could at least say farewell at her grave. He didn't make it back in time for the funeral, but he wouldn't have been allowed to attend, anyway. Annabell's father turned out to be a vindictive person. He hadn't wanted this young man associated with his daughter in life, and he was determined to prevent it after her death as well. Knowing that he couldn't keep the sailor out of the cemetery and that the location of the family plot wouldn't be a secret, he had the grave sites for everyone in the family dug, only with Annabell's deeper, so that her coffin could be covered with enough open space above it to make it look empty like those that really were, so that for the sailor it would be impossible to tell which was Annabell's grave. All the brokenhearted sailor could do was weep beside the family plot, not knowing exactly where in it Annabell lay. Today, some believe, Annabell wanders in the cemetery at night, searching for her lover, proving that love can be stronger than death.

But if it is Annabell, she may not be wandering alone. Another graveyard apparition has become a standard

Charleston story. The ghost of Mary Bloomfield Whitridge, who lived more than a century ago in the Charleston area, is known locally as the "Lady in White." According to some accounts, she walks in the graveyard every single evening. One tour guide, who led groups through the graveyard regularly and told its stories, never took any of it seriously until the evening he and his group of twenty tourists were gathered near Whitridge's grave and he saw a figure nearby, watching them. What unnerved him was that she watched everyone in the group closely, and no matter how people moved, her eyes followed them.

Folks who see her report an obviously female figure— some say fully formed, some say diaphanous and glowing, always in white, always moving. They believe she is looking for her husband, Edward Whitridge, now long dead of course, but not buried in the Unitarian cemetery. In fact, no one is sure just where he is buried. Mary and her husband had a long and happy marriage. They liked to walk together and sometimes strolled through the churchyard in the evening. But as they aged they began to have health problems that curtailed their walks. Mary became weak and felt faint after the mildest physical exertion; Edward had some kind of respiratory trouble. He smoked cigarettes he rolled himself from his own tobacco blend. Nobody thought much about smoking back then. Tobacco was a Southern crop, and lots of men used it. The notion that smoking could cause lung cancer, heart disease, and emphysema had not occurred to people yet, so Edward smoked for most of his life, becoming increasingly short of breath as he got older.

One day, Edward boarded a ship and sailed for Baltimore— some say to consult a physician there, though others believe he went on business. Ultimately, the distinction doesn't much matter: He suffered a heart attack and died on the way, so Mary never heard from him again after he sailed away.

Sadly, she never even heard what happened to him. Officials at the morgue in Baltimore had sent her a letter, but when they received no response, they buried him in Baltimore in a pauper's grave. According to the Macy and Buxton account, Mary died of heart failure on the very same day as her husband. But another version of the story tells us that she grieved over his absence for a long time and still had no idea what happened to him when she passed away, heartbroken. Either way, Mary's death is recorded officially as January 23, 1907 (see www.findagrave.com). She is buried in the fenced-in Whitridge family plot, next to Edward's empty grave in the Unitarian Church graveyard. Now she walks and walks, still looking for the husband she loved, in the graveyard where they used to stroll.

Chapter 10

Grief and Fright

St. Philip's Episcopal Churchyard
142 Church Street

*A photographer with a pre-digital camera took some photo-
graphs from outside the fence of the churchyard when it was
nearly dark. Later, he discovered the image of a woman in white
kneeling at a grave, even though no one had been there when he
took the picture. Two other apparitions sometimes appear in the
cemetery as well.*

The church was first built in 1670 on the site where St.
Michael's Episcopal Church stands today. The building was
finished in this location in 1724, burned in 1835, and was
rebuilt by 1838. During the Civil War, the church bells were
melted and turned into cannons, and not until 1976 were
new bells installed in the steeple. Historically significant
men are buried in the churchyard: John C. Calhoun, who
was vice president of the United States from 1825 to 1832;
Edward Rutledge, who signed the Declaration of Independence; and Charles Pinckney, a signer of the Constitution.

The church actually has two distinct burial grounds.
The one by the church was known as the "Friendly" graveyard, where only church members native to Charleston
were buried, while the "Strangers" graveyard was across the
street, the final resting place for church members not born
in Charleston. Even as important a man as John Calhoun
was laid to rest in the Strangers yard because he was born

in Abbeville. He did make it into Friendly, at least for a while, despite having been in favor of the Southern states' withdrawal from the Union. Because he was a secessionist, Charlestonians worried that Union troops would desecrate his grave with the same disregard they'd shown in burning buildings throughout the South, so they dug him up and moved his remains to an unmarked grave in the Friendly graveyard, where Yankees probably wouldn't find him.

After the war, members of the church insisted that Calhoun be returned to his original grave on the proper side of the street for those not native to Charleston. With all that moving around, it wouldn't be surprising if Calhoun said he'd had enough and let his spirit wander at will. But nobody has ever cited a Calhoun haunt. Indeed, all the important gentlemen on both sides of the street seem to stay buried and quiet. It's the women who seem restless. The photograph of a ghostly female figure in the graveyard tickles the imagination and attracts folks to ghost tours, inspires television shows, and gives guides plenty to talk about.

Harry Reynolds, a local photographer, took the picture in 1987, long before digital cameras, whose settings can be changed easily for varying light conditions. His camera was a modest one, loaded with a roll of Kodak ASA 200, the film most people used and the usual speed for daytime outdoor photography in those days. Reynolds had spent the day shooting the classic architectural sites in the French Quarter. Now it was getting dark, and he was ready to head home, but he still had a few shots left at the end of the roll. Like any serious photographer, he decided to finish the roll with some unplanned shots.

St. Philip's graveyard seemed like an interesting change of pace from all those buildings. The cemetery was fenced in and the gates were locked to prevent vandalism, but Reynolds found a place in the fence through which he could fit his camera to get a good view of some of the headstones. He ran off the rest of his film and went home pleased with a long day's work. When he picked up his pictures and negatives from the processor a few days later, he was pleased to see that some of the graveyard images looked good.

But when he got to the last picture he'd shot that day, something seemed wrong. He saw the translucent shape of what appeared to be a woman in a long cloak kneeling in front of one of the gravestones. She appeared to be translucent but fully formed, and her posture was definitely one of kneeling. Reynolds figured somebody had played a joke by messing with the negative, so he sent the film to Kodak to see how it could have been done. But the Kodak company replied that the image was definitely part of the photo as he'd shot it; nobody had tampered with the film, nor was it a double exposure.

It was the kind of thing that left one wondering whether to be frightened or amazed or curious. Because Reynolds was always curious about his surroundings, he started researching the grave and the story of the person who was buried there. It took a long time to gather the historical information, but Reynolds eventually learned that it was Susan Howard Hardy, wife of Gaston Hardy. They were well-to-do and respected in Charleston; they had a nice life. But all that changed after Susan Hardy became pregnant and gave birth to a stillborn baby. Childbirth could be a life-threatening ordeal in the 1800s, and just six days after her baby died without ever having lived, a heartbroken, grieving Susan Hardy died of peritonitis. She was only twenty-nine years old.

Reynolds's research revealed that his photo was taken exactly ninety-nine years after the death of Susan's child. Some say that she kneels at the grave mourning not her own death but the child who died before it came into the world. That might explain why pregnant women walking past the cemetery have sometimes felt ill and fearful and tend to hurry on by.

✛

And then there's the young woman in a party dress who wanders around a tall, leaning tombstone in the cemetery. Sally Ann may have become a ghost in an attempt to demonstrate that she did not believe in ghosts and that she certainly wasn't afraid of going where they were said to roam. The young woman and a group of her friends, who were waiting outside for a dance to begin in the hall next door to the church, began entertaining each other with stories about the ghost of Boney, "The Gray Man," a freed slave.

Boney's story begins long ago, when the church caught fire in 1796. Boney quickly climbed up on the roof to pull burning embers away from the steeple and toss them to the ground before the fire could spread. His action saved the church, and he was freed for his heroism. In one of life's tragic coincidences, the church caught fire again in 1835 and nobody could save it; however, it was rebuilt just three years later. By then Boney had come to consider this his place, and although nobody knows when he died, they say he continues to spend time around the church and thinks of the space as his own. People have reported seeing his ghost lounging about the graveyard, leaning against headstones, and making it clear he does not want intruders in his space.

He spends a lot of time around one tall, leaning tombstone in particular, and this is where he is most often seen.

The young people waiting for the ball to begin entertained each other with stories about how Boney would chase away anyone who dared to get near his favorite spot after dark. Sally Ann said, "Fiddlesticks. There's no such thing as ghosts, except in imagination." She probably believed it. She was a pretty, popular girl, though, who earned a little extra attention by disagreeing with the rest of her party. "I'll show you," she said. "I'll walk into the graveyard right now. I'll go up to the leaning tombstone and then I will come back, and there will not be any ghosts." The group laughed a little nervously. Some of them didn't think it was a good idea at all, but the more they objected, the more Sally Ann insisted she was going in.

"Maybe you'll say you went to the stone when you really didn't," one young man suggested. So, it was agreed that she would take his walking stick with her and plant it by the tombstone to prove she'd been there. And off she went, walking briskly with her long skirt swirling around her to prove she was not afraid. As she got closer to the leaning stone, she felt a little nervous. She felt as though she wasn't alone, but she knew nobody had followed her into the graveyard. As she approached the stone, she felt more and more frightened. She tried to call for her friends but couldn't make a sound. She wanted to run but couldn't move.

Sally Ann's friends laughed and joked and flirted for a while after she walked away, but when she didn't come back after a reasonable amount of time, they started to worry. Hoping there would be safety in numbers, the whole group hurried into the cemetery and headed directly to the leaning tombstone. To their horror, she was lying there, dead, with the walking stick pinned through her gown into the earth. Was that what had kept her from running away? Surely it couldn't have taken much strength to pull loose, especially if she'd been scared. But young women of that era didn't tend to be athletic and strong.

Even if she couldn't get free, though, what could have killed her? Is it possible that Sally Ann was literally frightened to death by an apparition?

Part Three

SCARY PLACES

The Old City Jail and the Exchange Building and Dungeon were the scenes of such horror in Charleston's early history that just hearing about what happened in those places is pretty frightening. No question, if ghosts hang around where they suffered when they were alive, the jail and the dungeon must be as full of spirits now as they were packed with inmates—slaves, criminals, out-of-favor politicians, and pirates—before death. Historians say that some of the people who died in these places were innocent of the crimes for which they had been incarcerated. People who take the tours report a variety of uncomfortable sensations, from feeling too hot to feeling chilled, and feeling the hair on their arms bristle. Even tour guides say they get uneasy entering these places—and that the spirits here are not benign.

Chapter 11

Touch Someone Else, Not Me

Old City Jail
21 Magazine Street and 17 Franklin Street

The site of the Old City Jail was a four-acre square of land set apart for public use by the planners of the city of Charleston. Bad things happened there even before the jail itself was built. Earlier structures included a workhouse for runaway slaves and a poorhouse. The jail was built in 1802 and was used as such until 1930, housing hardened criminals, pirates, runaway slaves, and the serial killers John and Lavinia Fisher until they were hanged. Reported hauntings range from clanking chairs and orbs of light to the figure of a woman walking through stone walls and cell bars.

George Hambrick, a young reporter from the *Charleston City Paper,* wasn't all that inclined to be spooked by the idea of ghosts or spirits or haunts. When the Southern Paranormal Investigation and Research team decided to investigate Charleston's Old City Jail, often called the most haunted site in the city, he volunteered to go along for the story—not as part of a big tour but with the investigating team.

At first, things seemed calm enough. A tour guide described the building as never having had running water and being "the coldest building in winter and the hottest building in summer." From a small group of other guides, he learned the stories that go with the standard walking tours.

But this tour, which began at midnight, was different. The investigation team already knew the stories. They wanted to see what, if anything, they could find when they went in to research the place. Apparitions? Voices? Orbs? What would they hear? Groans? Clanking chains?

As they went into the building and locked the gate behind themselves, Hambrick started getting a little uneasy. In a small room near the cells, he felt the hair on his arms rising at about the same time one of the team members said, "Did you feel that?" The team member then invited the spirit, if there was one, to make itself known by touching someone in the room. Hambrick devised a little mantra for possible spirit contacts: "Don't touch me. Touch someone else!" Later, cold air blew into the room as a team investigator told the story of a young black woman who was locked up, abused, and left for dead in this very space. In the end, the team left with more than a thousand photos, four hours of audio recordings, and many temperature and electromagnetic readings to analyze.

Other visitors to the jail have reported many unexplained events. During a renovation in 2000, some workers said they saw the apparition of a jailer with a rifle on the third floor. He passed through bars, then vanished. In 2006 people on a 10:00 p.m. tour heard the sounds of a dumbwaiter that doesn't work anymore moving from floor to floor.

Some reports go beyond the touching Hambrick wanted to avoid. The spirits can get physical, knocking sunglasses off the face of a man in the basement, making visitors and guides feel choked and out of breath, violently pushing and shoving visitors. A wheelchair dating from the 1820s kept on the premises never accumulates dust and often shows signs of recent use. Sometimes it's been known to bump into people during tours, apparently on purpose.

The history of the place invites the possibility of many, varied spirits, none of them happy. From the time it was built in 1790 until 1939, more than ten thousand people died here. Conditions were deplorable. Cells were packed with so many people that they could barely move. Sick prisoners were shoved into the same spaces as healthy ones. Slaves were often worked to death.

In 1822 Denmark Vesey, one of the founders of the Emanuel A.M.E. Church, was accused of organizing a rebellion of slaves in Charleston. When the plot was discovered, more than three hundred slaves and free blacks were arrested along with four white men. Vesey and thirty-five others were executed. After the failure of the rebellion and Vesey's execution, all black seamen who came into Charleston Harbor were forced to stay in the jail, even though they had been accused of no crime. During the Civil War, both Confederate and Federal prisoners of war were kept in the jail too, living in the same miserable conditions as the criminals and slaves.

For many years, people have claimed to see a black man in tattered old clothes wandering slowly down the halls, seemingly unaware of his surroundings or of living people around him. They suppose he was one of the slaves who was worked to death here and somehow moved on. They call this spirit a "residual haunting," which occurs when a spirit has been trapped in the loop of a terrible event that repeats over and over.

Some visitors, tour guides, and folks who have worked at the jail have reported foul odors, feeling ill and short of breath, and feeling choked. Perhaps it is the anger and misery of prisoners who have never passed on from this world, expressing their anger about their jailhouse experiences physically.

Being a guard here wasn't much better than being a prisoner, because guards were exposed to the same conditions as the prisoners, even if on the other side of the bars. The jail's history is no secret, and many people believe that the violence they sometimes feel here stems from the spirits of both prisoners who seek revenge against the authorities who locked them up and of guards angry over having been forced to work in such awful conditions. For instance, a set of keys has disappeared during a guided tour, mysteriously reappearing in an envelope stuffed through the mail slot later. Could that be the work of a miserable prison guard, reminding visitors that, back in the day, the Old Jail was no place to visit for fun?

But it's Lavinia Fisher, often called America's first female serial killer, who leads the cast of ghosts. Charlestonians have been telling stories about her for almost two hundred years. Lavinia and her husband, John, ran a hostelry called Six Mile House outside Charleston. It was, no surprise, just six miles outside Charleston. One story claims that she used her beauty to lure wealthy male guests into her parlor, where she offered them tea spiked with a touch of poison. Then, as a man grew groggy from his poisoned tea, she and John would help him to bed. Later, John would spring a trapdoor that tossed the bed and its occupant into a pit below the house, after which he would take whatever valuables the man carried, hoist the bed back into place, and get rid of the body.

But one night another John, John Peoples, stopped in. For some reason, instead of drinking his tea, he sneaked it into a houseplant and therefore went to his room feeling quite well. Because he wasn't drugged, or even sleepy yet, he sat in a chair by the door and soon watched in terror as the bed he might have been sleeping in fell through a trapdoor in the floor. He did what any smart guy would do: jumped out a window and ran all six miles to Charleston to tell the police. As they investigated, they heard reports of many travelers who had gone missing in that six-mile area, and they soon found bodies to confirm the reports.

That's the usual story in Charleston, but Todd Atteberry, who has made a career of investigating and writing about ghost stories and legends, as well as photographing their sites (www.gothichorrorstories.com), discovered another story. In this version, John and Lavinia still ended up in the Old Jail, but the details of how that happened are different. In Atteberry's version, Charleston police heard about robberies on the highway near Six Mile House. Robbery was considered almost worse than murder because, according to Atteberry, "Charleston lived and breathed commerce, and the highways were of vital importance." So robbers who got caught got hanged.

The police kicked the Fishers out of Six Mile House and left one Dave Ross to watch the place, figuring they'd get back to the Fishers later. But the next day a bunch of toughs, probably associated with John and Lavinia, broke in and hauled Ross outside, probably to beat him up or worse. He saw the beautiful Lavinia there, looking sweet, and he begged her for help.

This might have been an opportunity for her to demonstrate innocence, but she responded instead by trying to choke Ross and mash his face into a window. A little later the gang found John Peoples—the John Peoples who did *not* die in bed of poison—on the road and stole forty dollars from him. But they didn't kill him. He was glad not to be dead, of course, but forty dollars is a lot of money, so he went to the police to report the robbery. His story, along with that of Dave Ross, was enough to convict John and Lavinia of highway robbery. They ended up in an upper-floor room of the jail together, waiting for the noose.

John was able to crawl out a window and get to the ground. He probably would have escaped, but when Lavinia couldn't get out as well, he didn't resist capture and was put back inside. She was very beautiful, after all, and he had been a devoted partner. In any case, Lavinia didn't expect to hang because South Carolina law at the time did not allow married women to be put to death.

The judge, Elihu Bay, was old and deaf with a severe stutter, but he had no trouble pronouncing the couple guilty. Either the judge wasn't swayed by beauty or he had a mean streak, because he announced that John would hang first, leaving Lavinia widowed. It was legal to hang widows.

The couple tried every trick they knew to escape the sentence. They even secured a respite from the governor in the name of needing more time to prepare spiritually for death. Dr. Richard Furman, for whom Furman University is named, came to the prison every day to pray with John and Lavinia. But in the end, time ran out.

At first it looked as though John would accept his fate without protest, even claiming Lavinia had no part in the crimes—his final attempt to protect her. He went quietly to the gallows without resisting. But at the last minute, he shouted out that he was innocent, that this was all a mistake. And then, maybe hoping to get right with God, he changed his mind again and asked to be forgiven for his crimes. But the hanging went on.

Widow Lavinia had her own plan for staying alive. The day she was to be hanged, she wore a wedding dress to the gallows, hoping that some man in the crowd would be so affected by her sorry state and her beauty that'd he'd marry her on the spot and make her a wife once again, not a widow.

It didn't work. No man came forward offering to marry her. Maybe they were afraid of ending up like all those traveling men who had been seduced by her beauty and wound up dead. The scene ended with Lavinia being dragged up on the gallows, struggling, screaming, and cursing. The crowd was stunned by her rage and also by her vocabulary. Damning everybody was not the language of a beautiful woman, even one about to be hanged. Where did she learn those awful words? Who knew someone so beautiful could shriek and scream like that? They say that Lavinia's last words were, "If you have a message you want to send to hell, give it to me—I'll carry it."

But she's still around, they say, because she was so vile even the devil wouldn't take her. Some people believe that the female spirit seen wandering among the tombstones in the graveyard of Charleston's Unitarian Church is Lavinia, though it's hard to imagine why she would be in that particular place, not really bothering anybody. Lavinia and John Fisher were buried in a field near the Old Jail, and according to the reports of visitors and guides, she prowls around the jail, not the churchyard.

Some people experience her presence while they're inside the building. Others, from the outside, say they've seen her through the window, still cursing and vowing revenge. You don't hear about anybody actually going on in after having seen that.

Chapter 12
Angry Spirits

Old Exchange Building and Provost Dungeon
122 East Bay Street

Charlestonians will say that this site represents the best and the worst of Charleston's history. It is owned now by the South Carolina Society of the Daughters of the American Revolution, operated as a history museum with exhibits and guided tours. Nobody seems to have any trouble with the main floors, but many visitors to the dungeon below have had scary experiences, as have some of the guides.

Although docents in the Old Exchange Building lead tours of Provost Dungeon during the day, some people want the extra thrill of a night tour led by a professional guide. Joyce and her friends were in Charleston for a wedding the next day, and everybody was in full tourist mode. Her friends wanted to go on one of the night tours. Joyce thought the whole ghost thing was a lot of commercial hooey, but the rest of her friends had talked about it over lunch and were so enthusiastic that she went along, mellowed by a great crab cake sandwich and a generous pour of white wine. She thought the tour was a waste of money, but she wasn't about to spoil the mood.

At the dungeon, their guide led them through the front door, past a half-full pit of water, talking about what it was like to be in this prison during colonial and revolutionary days, when pirates, patriots, criminals, prostitutes, and other women in chains were all crammed together—healthy and sick alike—with inadequate food, dreadful sanitation, no medical care, and little hope of ever getting out, except possibly to be hanged. At first Joyce's friends giggled, but as they heard the stories and saw the exhibits, complete with mannequins depicting dungeon life, they became subdued. This wasn't funny.

Still, Joyce thought, that didn't mean the place was haunted. It was uncomfortable, though—too hot. She was sweating. Southern girls once were raised to believe that ladies did not sweat or even perspire (they *glistened*), but this was a most unladylike situation. She was sweating profusely and having trouble breathing too.

Then she heard what sounded like a woman moaning, but she couldn't see anybody who might be making the sound. She decided not to say anything about any of this because nobody else was sweating; in fact, one of the girls said the place was freezing cold. And no one else appeared to hear anything unusual.

Joyce got through the rest of the tour in a daze, hardly hearing the guide and not looking closely at the exhibits for fear of seeing something weird. It wasn't until the group was back outside that Joyce began to feel cool and breathe easily again. She didn't say anything at all. She didn't know what had happened to her during the dungeon tour, but she couldn't pooh-pooh the possibility that it was haunted anymore. (Some tour guides have said it's often the skeptics who have spooky experiences on these tours.)

By then the whole gang was subdued, and one of them said she was glad the wedding was in a church and not at the Old Exchange Building. The wedding could have been held in the Old Exchange Building, though. It is a popular place for all kinds of special celebrations, including weddings. After the museum closes at 5:00 p.m., the Old Exchange offers several rooms, including the Great Hall, with some requirements for keeping the number of musicians low and using reliable caterers for food. For an extra fee, you can arrange a private tour of the dungeon below if guests are interested in haunted places. Some people say the spirits of dungeon prisoners linger, even though the dungeon was abandoned for many years and only reopened as a tour exhibit in 1966, after a lot of renovation. But apparently the spirits stay down in the dungeon and don't venture into the upper stories of living quarters and museum exhibits.

The Old Exchange is considered one of the most architecturally and historically important buildings in America— a center of contradiction. Here, in the splendid building, some of the country's most important meetings took place, forging the path to independence and democracy. At the same time, the slave trade was in full swing just outside, and conditions in the dungeon beneath the building were inhuman. The British built the exchange between 1767 and 1771, primarily as a place of customs and business, serving the lively commercial trade port town. The most profitable trade was in rice, indigo, and slaves from Africa. The first level was an open trading space, while the next floor accommodated offices and an assembly room. Cellars below those floors were for storage. The dungeon, with its arched brick ceiling, held a variety of prisoners in conditions so bad that many died awaiting punishment or execution.

When the colonists demanded independence from the crown, British troops moved into Charles Town in 1780. They controlled the city and the exchange until 1782. During those years they threw active patriots, including three signers of the Declaration of Independence, into the dungeon with criminals. Some Revolutionaries escaped by signing a loyalty oath to the king of England, while others were hanged for treason. In 1791 US President George Washington spent a week in Charleston. Banquets, a concert, and a ball in his honor were held in the Great Hall of the Old Exchange. He and the guests most certainly did not venture into the dungeon.

Despite its renovation for tours, this place scares many visitors. Some of the tour guides don't like it much, either. For one thing, seawater still seeps in and has to be pumped out regularly, so the place smells musty and moldy. Nobody can identify the spirits that hang around because usually they're not seen so much as they are felt and heard. Sometimes they cause objects to move.

The first place you come to as you go through the door is a pit containing the groundwater that leaks in. Some prisoners drowned in that pit, and one child on a tour knew about it intuitively before the guide told the story. Another visitor felt the area was unnaturally hot but didn't know that people had been burned to death here. At one time, indigo, a crop that thrived in the Lowcountry and was much in demand in the English textile industry, was stored in the pit, where a strange blue glow remains even now, adding to the spooky feeling of the dungeon. The domed brick ceiling gives some visitors a feeling that it is closing in on them.

The Old Exchange website says, "It is our goal to present the history of the Old Exchange in an interesting and informative manner. Young and old alike seem drawn to the Provost Dungeon. Our experienced docents will lead you through its eerie confines, and our animatronic storytellers—the Deputy Collector, Mister Mate and Tom the

Stockman—will entertain you and your family with wonderful tales of pirates and patriots. You'll be having so much fun, you may not want to leave!"

It does work that way for lots of visitors, but not for all—and not always for the tour guides, either. Suppose as you were walking though the dungeon hall, the chain across one exhibit started jerking back and forth—not the gentle swing of having been bumped, but a persistent, rhythmic movement that did not gradually slow down as a chain that had been touched by a tourist would? When this happened to one tourist, he called the rest of his group. As they watched, chains in front of other exhibits started behaving in the same manner, leaving the group surrounded by clanking chains. Their guide hustled everyone out without ceremony or apology. Outside, she told the group that she herself had heard groaning and that on another occasion something had pushed her backward as she opened the door.

Other times, people touring the dungeon have heard crying and moaning and seen lights swaying back and forth for no discernible reason. Some, like Joyce in the bridal party, experience difficulty breathing. And more than one tourist has claimed that the mannequins move their heads or follow people with their eyes.

Provost Dungeon has been called one of the worst prisons in United States history. It seems likely that many Charlestonians had no idea what really went on there, while those who did know likely believed that the criminals deserved extreme punishment. Almost certainly, some people who died in the dungeon were not guilty of the crimes for which they were imprisoned. Could it be that some of their spirits are still around, trying to make their stories known or seeking revenge for their mistreatment?

Part Four

HEARD BUT NOT SEEN, SEEN BUT NOT HEARD

Haunted places often have a variety of supernatural happenings. Some folks may see silent apparitions, for instance, while at the same place other people hear sounds but see nothing. But other sites have become famous for a singular, repeated event: sightings with no sound or often repeated sound but nothing to see. The ghost car on Cooper River Bridge is an example of a silent sighting, while the poltergeist orphans may be a case of a sound loop. One theory is that if ghosts are not attempting any interaction with living people, are visible but seem unaware of their surroundings, or are silent and repeating the same behavior over and over, they are trapped in the moment of their death. These haunts are doomed to repeat the same acts endlessly.

Chapter 13
The Whistling Doctor

59 Church Street and Dueler's Alley

If all the people who have shot it out in Dueler's Alley stayed around to haunt the scene, you wouldn't be able to move through the space because it would be too crowded with ghosts. Although they've left behind marks of their duels, they seem to stay dead and buried except for occasionally scratching at passersby. But one ghost, once a popular doctor, has hung around. People don't see him, but they hear the happy tune he whistled as he walked every day.

Joseph Brown Ladd was a young man, just in his early twenties, when he came to Charleston from his home in Rhode Island to practice medicine. Even though Dr. Ladd had experienced sadness in his life, he loved his work and he loved Charleston. He walked to work every day whistling, always the same tune. People came to expect it each morning and again each evening. After he died, still a young man, as the result of a silly duel, people still heard him whistling as clearly as if he were still walking to and from work every day.

That was in the 1780s, and anybody who could remember hearing him when he was alive has been gone a long time. But people still hear whistling, especially around the house at 59 Church Street, where he once lived, although nobody ever sees him. Some people hear whistling from his room on the second floor. Other folks hear whistling on the stairs he used to run down on his way to work. And some folks swear they hear him all along Church Street, where he used to walk. Nobody has ever *seen* the ghost of Dr. Ladd, but even children who don't know his story sometimes hear him and ask about it.

Dr. Ladd must have had a happy spirit to find his way to Charleston and enjoy being there. He left behind a family in Rhode Island, where he didn't really fit in. He was delicate of frame, loved reading and poetry—not exactly the kind of boy to suit a father who was trying to earn a living as a farmer. Indeed, it was his father who said that if Joseph insisted on earning a living with his brain rather than his hands, he'd have to learn medicine. That was certainly a better occupation for a young man who read poetry and even wrote it while hoeing the back forty. So Joseph agreed.

At least he did until he learned that to practice medicine, he would have to leave his hometown and his Amanda. Amanda was a gentle person, very pretty with her blond hair and blue eyes, also a lover of poetry, the perfect match for Joseph. They spent many hours together, and soon all the poetry Joseph wrote was for her. Unfortunately, they met after Amanda's father died, leaving her the ward of a guardian who was living comfortably on Amanda's inheritance and refused to consent to her betrothal, which would have meant losing Amanda's fortune. But Amanda was no wimp. She said she would marry Joseph with or without permission.

The greedy guardian and some of his family set out to secure Amanda's money for themselves by spreading terrible rumors about Joseph Brown Ladd, maligning not only his character but also his medical competence. Not everybody believed the stories of course—certainly Amanda did not—but it became obvious that he could not practice in a community that did not trust him. He hadn't yet the means to support a wife, so Joseph sadly headed off to establish his practice in Charleston without Amanda.

In Charleston, when he got out of the carriage on the outskirts of the town, he was rumpled and tired and needed a place to spend the night. A man standing in the doorway of a tavern there stepped forward to warn Joseph away from the hostelry his driver had recommended. The man was Ralph Isaacs, a husky but intelligent-looking man. He introduced himself to Joseph and, after hearing that Joseph had come to town to set up a medical practice, offered to go with him to a safe tavern at the corner of Board and Church Streets for a decent meal.

Driving through the city, Joseph was shocked by the damage the recent war had done to all the buildings and streets, but he enjoyed listening to Isaacs's account of the city and its people. He felt as though he'd already made a friend. Isaacs liked Joseph too and was happy to be on friendly terms with a doctor, a man of status.

With Isaacs's help, Joseph carried a letter from General Nathaniel Greene, who had earned prestige fighting in the Charleston area during the war. The letter recommended Joseph as a boarder to two elderly sisters, Fannie and Dellie Rose, friends of the general. It was a beautiful house on Church Street, not far from the tavern, and Joseph was delighted when the sisters immediately offered him a room upstairs, doing all they could to make sure he would be comfortable and happy there. Joseph liked the sisters. They doted on him because he brightened the mood of the entire house. They loved to hear him run down the stairs in the morning and back up at the end of his day, always whistling an old tune they'd never heard before. It was a happy time.

Joseph's medical practice flourished, and his friendship with Isaacs was a pleasant diversion for a man new to the community. Of course Joseph still pined for Amanda. He wrote and sent her many poems expressing all the traits he loved about her, looking ahead to the time when he would be able to send for her to join him in Charleston as his wife. Sometimes Isaacs could not understand why Joseph wanted to spend time in the evening mooning in his room writing poetry, when they could have gone to a tavern together. Quickly becoming known around town as the handsome new Dr. Ladd, Joseph was included in more and more activities of people with a high place in local society. Because Isaacs could never hope for anything similar, he began resenting what he saw as Joseph's privilege, even though the two men still spent time together. Their last really good time together was at a rollicking concert in the old Exchange Building. It wasn't until the night of the opening of a Shakespeare play at a venue called Harmony House that the relationship went really sour.

The play was *Richard III*, featuring Mr. Godwin, a respected actor from Savannah. In fact, it was this actor who established Harmony House, partly because he thought it would be profitable and partly to assure a place where he, himself, could perform—as Richard, in this case. Queen Anne was played by a Miss Barrett, a pretty young actress who had also recently arrived in Charleston. Although she didn't have much acting experience, she was shapely, and critics predicted a bright future for her in Charleston.

Even before the performance began, Isaacs was feeling churlish because he saw Joseph, beautifully dressed, sitting in a box laughing and chatting with some of society's well-known and well-to-do men and women. Isaacs had to sit on a lower level, knowing he could never aspire to anything more; Charleston was a very class-conscious city. The evening was hot and humid, especially in the theater, which didn't help Isaacs's mood. As it turned out, poor Queen Anne's performance was no match for that of King Richard. Her voice wasn't strong, and, really, she was too inexperienced to have been asked to tackle a role like Queen Anne. Even so, this was entertainment with the promise of many more shows to come, and a pretty girl is a pleasure even if you can't hear most of her lines. Despite how hot the theater was, people mingled at intermission in good humor.

Except for Isaacs. Though Joseph greeted him, friendly as ever, Isaacs responded rudely, observing that Joseph, "the hifalutin Dr. Ladd," was now keeping company with fine friends and wouldn't be mingling anymore with common people like him. Intermission was over before any real discussion could follow, and Joseph was left baffled by Isaacs's sudden hostility.

After the show, Joseph waited for Isaacs so they could walk home together. This was probably a mistake, because Isaacs was still hot, tired, embarrassed by his lower class status, and generally in a foul mood. Although he often had been a good conversationalist, on this night he would do no more than mutter.

The only time he responded with any energy was after Joseph had praised the performance of King Richard. Isaacs attacked Miss Barrett for an inadequate performance and was quite nasty about it. He said that she had mumbled her lines, moved stiffly, and used her hands in a few unnatural gestures over and over. According to Isaacs, she was not fit to be on a public stage, and she should never be allowed there again.

Joseph pointed out that she was still learning the performance arts and must have been intimidated working with a well-known, much-admired actor in a role she'd never played before. She deserved encouragement and a chance to develop her skills. Isaacs started to rant, saying sarcastically that of course his opinion would not matter since he was lowborn. Joseph tried to smooth over the disagreement, reassuring Isaacs that their differences would seem trivial by next morning.

But Isaacs wouldn't quit. In the days that followed, he began spreading rumors about Joseph's moral character and professional competence. It was all beginning to seem too much like his earlier experience in Rhode Island, and when his friends urged him to refute Isaacs's charges, Joseph reluctantly published a statement in the local newspaper, calling his friendship with Isaacs an "unfortunate mistake." The quarrel escalated, until friends insisted that in the interests of his own honor, Joseph Ladd must challenge Ralph Isaacs to a duel.

That sounds like an extreme reaction to a personal disagreement these days, but at the time in England, duels were an accepted way of settling serious disputes. The colonists had brought the custom over from England. The practice of dueling followed written rules and was looked upon as an honorable way to prevent ongoing vendettas.

According to some tales, Dr. Ladd challenged Isaacs to the duel in response to a letter Isaacs had published in the newspaper attacking not only the doctor but also the actress and poet Mary "Perdita" Robinson. Robinson was famous for her role as Perdita in the play *A Winter's Tale,* commissioned by the Prince of Wales in 1779. It was said that she had turned away Isaacs's affections in favor of Dr. Joseph Ladd.

In this version of the story, the letter maligned "Perdita" for immoral behavior. Under the codes of dueling and honor in those days, it would have been Dr. Ladd's obligation to duel in response to a direct insult to a woman "under a gentleman's care." This story has elements of believability. Mary Robinson was a beautiful woman, a successful stage actress, and easy with her affections. And she wrote poetry. It's not hard to imagine that "Perdita" and Dr. Ladd might have become involved.

On the other hand, let's not forget Amanda. Storyteller Margaret Rhett Martin tracked down a copy of *The Literary Remains of Joseph Brown Ladd, M.D.* by Mrs. Elizabeth Hawkins (published by H. C. Sleight in 1832). Martin quotes Ladd's poems extensively in her book, *Charleston Ghosts.* Apparently Joseph wrote poems for Amanda until the night before the duel, assuring her that no matter what happened she must remember him as her distant lover, even though he might never return to her. Was he not only predicting his own demise but also promising his enduring presence, at least in spirit?

Poor Joseph approached the early-morning encounter still hoping for some way to reestablish a relationship with his one-time friend and avoid tragedy. He'd had little experience with guns or fighting. But the grim process went on, with Isaacs refusing the offer of a less-lethal encounter with swords.

The men went through all the motions of a classic duel, marching twenty paces apart, turning, firing. Joseph simply could not kill another person deliberately. He was a doctor, and a doctor's mission was to save lives, not end them. He fired into the ground—or into the air, according to some. And then he waited, perhaps expecting some such courtesy in return. According to the rules, a duel must be fought until one of the men either died or was wounded so seriously judges stopped the fight. Isaacs fired low, hitting Joseph in the knee or, by some accounts, fired twice, hitting him first in one knee, then the other. Was his aim bad, or was he, like Joseph, trying to find a way to spare a life? Or was he intent on crippling Joseph for life? Whatever he'd meant to do, the judges ended the duel and the wounded man was carried back to his room, where Miss Fannie and Miss Dellie did what they could to dress his wounds and make him comfortable, coaxing him to eat enough to build up his strength. But he grew steadily weaker and often was delirious, calling for Amanda. The sisters tried to contact her so that she could come to him, but her guardian was taking no chances and kept her under guard day and night. Joseph languished for weeks. Then one morning the sisters heard him whistling and climbed the stairs as fast as they could. They hurried into his room expecting to see him feeling better. Instead, they found him dead.

From that day on, people have heard Joseph whistling. Some hear him in what is popularly called "Dueler's Alley," though the real name is Philadelphia Alley. So many duels have been fought here that some people who walk the cobblestones say they smell gunsmoke and hear pistol shots. But it is where Joseph used to live, the soft yellow house at 59 Church Street, that he is heard most often. Sometimes, when children ask where the sound is coming from, their parents tell them that a person in a nearby yard is whistling at the birds.

One observer has another notion. The house at Church Street is a private residence now, with a plaque out front featuring an old newspaper clipping telling the doctor's story. But the reporter who wrote it must have been in a hurry, or in his cups, because in the story, the doctor's name is written as "Joseph Ladd Brown." This observer suggests that Dr. Joseph Brown Ladd might be indignant that the newspaper got his name wrong, and he just wants the sign to be fixed. What if the good doctor really is just whistling for attention until somebody corrects that mistake? Then would he slip quietly off into the next world?

Chapter 14

The Poltergeist
Pranksters

Joe E. Berry Residence Hall
College of Charleston
Corner of Calhoun and St. Philip Streets

The Joe E. Berry Residence Hall, built in 1988, stands on the earlier site of the Charleston Orphan House that was torn down in 1951. Four children died, probably from smoke inhalation, during a fire at the orphanage in 1918. Students and their parents who have stayed in the dorm built on the old site say that those children are still around, playing jokes, making noise in the building, and singing—especially late at night.

Lots of colleges have stories about ghosts that haunt the campus, so when Suzanna moved into the Berry dorm (which opened to freshmen in 1991) in 2011, she did not pay much attention to the talk about supernatural occurrences there. As she would tell you, rooms in Berry Hall are modest. Students have the use of kitchen and laundry facilities, designated study areas, a computer room, Internet access, and a cheery common area for special gatherings. Just not the kind of place one would expect to be haunted. But dorm residents over the years have reported the sounds of children singing late at night, rattling doors, and, most often, someone setting off fire alarms when there is no fire.

The story starts long before Suzanna was born. The orphanage was established in 1790, providing a home not only for children with no living parents but also sometimes for those whose parents could not keep them. Discipline was strict but not cruel, and children who lived there were provided nourishing food, adequate clothing, and as much comfort as the busy staff could provide.

In the autumn of 1918, an epidemic of Spanish influenza struck the children of the orphanage, taxing the staff as they struggled to keep seriously ill children alive. This left little time for the ones who did not get sick. Those children were sent outside to play, where they could wear off energy and were less exposed to the contagious disease. With the attention of the adults so focused on the very sick children, pranks that ordinarily would have gotten the healthy kids into trouble went unnoticed, or at least unremarked.

It was one such prank that led to the death of four of the ill orphans and is the basis of the paranormal events reported at the Berry dorm almost a century later. The healthy kids were playing outside, making "tents" from cardboard boxes, pretending to camp like those lucky guys they saw in pictures from orphanages in the Blue Ridge Mountains. Those orphans were camping, fishing, and tossing rocks into the streams. It didn't take much youthful imagination to see the boxes as tents, but what the orphanage staff saw looked like an enclave of homeless people littering the area—not at all appropriate for the broad yards around the large, gothic orphanage, which was architecturally spectacular.

Ordinarily children who were caught scrounging boxes from the trash were taken inside and reprimanded. But with all the adults focused on caring for the sick kids, the well ones, who probably did not fully understand the gravity of what was happening inside, got away with building their tent city. One has to wonder if they were craving some adult attention, even if only the disciplinary kind, for they must have believed that their scheme would draw attention.

The children moistened one of their cardboard tents with some damp mud around the bottom, then set it on fire. The legend does not say where they would have managed to obtain matches. Their idea was to wait until the tent smoked, then see who came out to investigate. The cardboard tent did smoke, but nobody in the building had time to notice and come out right then, so while the youngsters waited, the fire burned higher. The wind blew. The fire spread to other tents, and then to the orphanage itself, where it did not burn extensively but instead poured billows of smoke into the building. The already exhausted staff began carrying ill children, some two hundred of them, out of the building. Somehow, four got left behind. Already unwell and possibly asleep or even unconscious, they probably died from smoke and fume inhalation without realizing what was happening.

Later stories suggest that the children never realized they were dead, so they just hung around, kids forever, laughing, singing, playing jokes, and feeling much better than they had when they were alive and ill. If the stories are true, the children would have seen tremendous changes in the place they had known as home before they could move into "their" building again to confound College of Charleston officials, renovation crews, and successive generations of students at Berry dorm.

The orphanage was torn down in 1951 and replaced in 1978 by a private, nonprofit center, the California Youth Development Center, in North Charleston. For a few years a Sears Roebuck and Company store stood where the old orphan house had been, but the store soon failed and was also razed. The Joe E. Berry dorm was built toward the front of the site in 1988.

The legend does not say exactly when the poltergeist kids got there, nor whether the ghostly group consists of more than just the four orphans who died in the fire, though they are so noisy that is a possibility. In any event, strange things started happening soon after the freshman dorm, which was coed at the time, opened in 1991. Fire alarms went off, usually late at night, summoning the local firefighters, who always hustled the students out of the building and then went through every room looking for fire or even smoke, never finding either. The problem grew increasingly worrisome, not only because the fire company began levying fines against the college for false alarms but also because of the possibility that students would eventually ignore the alarms at a time when there really was a fire. The fire marshal questioned the students over and over and even tried dusting the fire alarm boxes with a powder that under a black light would show up on the hands of anyone who had touched an alarm. No student ever glowed in the dark, and none ever admitted to pulling such stunts. But the alarms did not stop going off, either. The fire department suggested rewiring the dormitory's alarm system but also let the college know they still suspected student pranks.

School officials must have agreed, because in 1996 they decided to make the dorm all-female and house the freshman males elsewhere. Some of the freshman boys could be getting a kick out of rousing all the students, especially the girls, so that they had to huddle outside in whatever skimpy clothing they had on until the alarm was cleared. It's possible that some conservative old-school administrators had never been enthusiastic about coed dormitories anyway, so Joe E. Berry Hall has remained an all-female building since 1997.

At first it looked as though the move had worked. The frequency of the false alarms diminished. Then reports from female students and their parents introduced a new set of problems. The young women began to complain that, late at night, the building was full of what sounded like little kids laughing and singing, racing around in the halls and stairways and even outside in the courtyard. They said it sounded like more than four children. The girls could not get away from the sounds, which even rang through the air-conditioning vents. Parents who had been invited to spend a night in the dorm during summer break complained about children running wild in the halls late at night.

After reports surfaced of creaking noises and young voices singing "Ring around the Rosie" echoing through the air-conditioning vents, officials decided that perhaps the problem was in the heating, ventilation, and air-conditioning system (HVAC). It could be, they reasoned, that overactive imaginations heard "songs" that were really just pieces of metal rubbing together. In 2003 the Rosenblum Coe Architect firm renovated that system, taking out all the old hardware and putting in modern fittings and equipment. They also updated the fire alarm system.

On the ghostly scene, nothing changed. Students still heard unexplained noises in the building, and false fire alarms happened even more often than before. It was still happening in 2011, so often that even new resident Suzanna was beginning to believe something odd was going on.

The college kept trying new ways to stop the unexplained events. Some thought that significant remodeling would do the trick. Of course the work would not be just about getting rid of ghosts. Making the place comfortable and pleasant was important too. The rooms were getting worn; after all, even careful students can be hard on the buildings in which they live. Who knows what may have come loose somewhere in the walls or halls to cause all the ruckus?

So in 2012 the Brantly Construction Company undertook a $3 million renovation on Berry Hall, keeping crews working seven days a week to finish in just three months, in time for fall enrollment. The 2012 renovation included changes to allow more light in the building. The project introduced bright colors to decorate the rooms, hallways, and common areas. A sprinkler system and digital security cameras were installed.

College officials must have hoped all this change would put the old poltergeists to rest. Unfortunately, though, it did not. Although Suzanna, now a sophomore, no longer lived in the dorm, she remained curious enough to follow the stories of subsequent freshman classes living in Berry Hall. There was plenty to follow. In addition to the stories that passed from person to person on campus, the Internet began lighting up with anecdotes too.

On March 10, 2012, Carole St-Laurent posted an Internet message about a ghost tour led by Geordie Buxton, telling the familiar story of the orphanage, the fire, and the poltergeists at Berry Hall. When she went looking for more information, she found a February 2012 Facebook note that told another familiar story. The student wrote, "This is ridiculous. It's 5 a.m. and I am writing this from outside Berry Hall Dorm in 30 degree weather because the fire alarm has gone off for about the 3rd time this semester at some odd hour of the night. . . ." And there were not even any fresh-man males in the crowd to blame for enjoying a peep at the scantily clad young women who rushed out into the cold when the alarm sounded.

Also in March of that year, some residents of the dorm circulated a petition asking the college to refund some of their tuition money because of their experiences there. The issues included dorm water being turned off without notice and rooms being too hot for comfort, but many of the people who signed the petition cited that familiar old complaint: fire alarms going off frequently when there was no fire. Explana-tions in the early days blamed electrical work being done on the building, but long after those workers were gone, the alarms kept sounding. Students also complained that eleva-tors often did not work. Who knows whether mechanical problems or the poltergeists are to blame? And what about the time the door to the laundry room was locked for a week and, though the students reported it, nobody on the staff knew anything about it?

As for Suzanna, she no longer scoffs at the concept of poltergeists haunting the dorm, given her experiences and those of other young women she has known. As one of them told Natasha Gehilhausen, who was keeping a portfolio about the college on a website, in 2012: "I remember hearing about the hauntings at the dorm before I decided to live there a few years ago but I did not believe in ghosts or any supernatural mumbo jumbo. After spending an entire year at the dorm, my opinion has drastically changed. Ghosts are real. They may not be evil or demonic but they certainly are real."

That's all well and good for students who leave the school after a few years, but what about the administrators for whom coping with all the stories and events has become part of the job description? For them, convincing the poltergeist spirits to go away would be a blessing. But here's the question: Given how hard it is to get regular kids to wind down and go to bed at the end of a day, what would it take to get a bunch of undisciplined poltergeists, who apparently never get tired, to settle down and let regular people get on with their daily lives? If the poltergeist kids don't know they are dead, will they haunt the building forever?

Chapter 15
Strange Encounters

Cooper River Bridge

During stormy weather on February 24, 1946, the crew aboard the 12,000-ton ship Nicaragua Victory *mistakenly hauled up the ship's anchors instead of just taking up slack in the anchor chain as instructed, setting the freighter loose and out of control. The ship struck the main tower and a bottom support of the Cooper River Bridge. Almost at once, sections of the bridge fell into the water, leaving great gaps in the road. When the driver in one car couldn't stop soon enough, his automobile dropped into the water upside down, killing the family in the vehicle. Afterwards, until the old bridge was replaced in July 2005, some people crossing it reported seeing a ghost car, usually in February.*

It wasn't that Harriet had a lead foot, exactly. But she had recently moved to Charleston from "up North" (Charlotte, North Carolina), where people liked to move along at a brisk pace. And she drove a peppy new 1996 Honda Civic that handled like a dream, negotiating narrow spaces and stopping with a touch of the brake. So unlike folks in larger cars, she moved along the narrow, two-lane Cooper River Bridge, passing slower vehicles, up the incline to one of the trestles at highway speed, with ease. That was quite a feat, because the ascents to the trestle peaks and then the immediate descents had earned the bridge its nickname, "Roller-coaster Bridge."

Each vehicle ahead of Harriet climbed the steep road and then disappeared from her view as it went down the other side. Just after she had hit the gas to pass another slowpoke, she noticed something odd about the car. It was a green Oldsmobile, a really old one with a rounded back end unlike anything she'd seen on the road before. She slowed down to drive next to the Olds for a closer look, then immediately wished she had not. Through the windows of the old car, she saw five people dressed in the vintage clothing of the mid-1900s—a man and woman in the front and two children with an old lady in the backseat. They all looked dead, even though they were sitting upright. All of them were pale and unmoving. For a moment the driver seemed to turn his head toward Harriet, but his face was skeletal, with no expression.

So much for moving along briskly. Harriet slipped back into the right lane behind the Oldsmobile at reduced speed and watched as the antique car climbed the incline and then simply disappeared for good. As she descended from the steep peak, that old, slow Oldsmobile was gone.

Harriet wasn't the first person to see the ghostly Oldsmobile on the bridge. The stories began after a horrendous accident on the bridge in February 1946. When it was opened in 1929, this bridge was state of the art, about 2.7 miles long, rising 150 feet above the river. Building it took seventeen months and cost $6 million. The bridge was privately owned and cost drivers a fifty-cent toll to go across. In 1943 the state of South Carolina bought the bridge, eliminating the toll charge three years later. Without the money from those fees, wear and inadequate maintenance began to weaken the aging structure. And while once it had the highest clearance in the world, newer bridges were higher to accommodate larger, modern ships requiring greater clearance.

In 1946, however, the twelve-thousand-ton freighter *Nicaragua Victory* could have gone through okay had it not been for a combination of unfortunate incidents. The ship had been in an accident and was moored in Charleston Harbor, awaiting repair, when the weather grew stormy. The captain moved *Nicaragua Victory* from the harbor to a river location about a mile upstream from the bridge, where there was more protection from the weather. The crew shut down the engines and dropped anchor.

As the storm became more violent, a night captain ordered another anchor to be dropped. Then he told the crew to tighten up the slack in the anchor chain. Apparently he and the crew had a failure to communicate. Instead of just taking up slack in the chain, they pulled in both anchors, leaving the ship loose with no steering power because the engines were shut down. Completely at the mercy of the wind and water, the ship spun through the water toward the bridge, slamming into one of its main pillars and bottom support trestles. After a moment, huge sections of the bridge and its roadway broke off, dropping into the water and even onto the deck of the freighter. Within minutes, a huge gap in the roadway prevented anyone from driving across.

Bill and Dorothy Clapper's car stopped in time and was safe. Another car was not so lucky. The green Oldsmobile sedan hesitated at the commotion, slowed, and only gradually started forward again. Elmer Lawson, his wife, two young children, and their grandmother were in the car as it plunged, upside down, into the river below. If Elmer had sped ahead instead of slowing down and hesitating, they might have made it before the bridge fell away, living to tell a scary story about the day the Cooper River Bridge broke apart. The people in the car probably died quickly after the car dropped into the water. Searchers could find no sign of the Lawson family shortly after the disaster. It wasn't until almost two months later that a cleanup crew working near the bridge hoisted the car out of the water, with all five people still inside. Repairs to make the bridge usable again took six months.

It was another family of five crossing the bridge on their way to Charleston from a vacation on Sullivan's Island in 1966 who told the most dramatic story about the ghost car. As a conscientious man with his family in the car, the driver was careful but maintained a reasonable speed as he drove, paying close attention to the task because the wind was gusting wildly. Suddenly he came right up behind a slow-moving old car and slammed on his brakes to avoid hitting it. The man and his wife had time to notice that there were five people in the aged sedan, all dressed in old-fashioned clothes and not moving. Then it disappeared like a puff of smoke on a cloudy day.

Over the years, other drivers have reported similar sightings, always noting that the Oldsmobile seemed to jerk to a stop, then move again, slowly, in a pattern similar to the action that had doomed the Lawsons when the bridge failed.

Ultimately the old Cooper River Bridge, also known as John P. Grace Memorial Bridge in honor of Charleston's former mayor, had to be taken down because it was not only unsafe but also inadequate to handle both highway and river traffic. It was replaced by the Arthur Ravenel Jr. Bridge in 2005. Today the phantom Lawson family appears to have been crowded out by the new eight-lane bridge. Or could it be that once the old bridge where they met disaster was gone, they were finally able to move on to the next life?

Chapter 16
Gray Man's Warning

Pawley's Island

The famous Gray Man may be South Carolina's most well-meaning ghost. People see him, usually walking silently on the beach, just before bad weather moves in. They see him but hear nothing other than the sounds of the ocean. He has been around, warning people about danger from oncoming storms, since 1822—long before the National Weather Service, TV weather reports, and the Emergency Broadcast System. His appearances have been said to save not only lives but also, mysteriously, homes on Pawley's Island.

In the Gullah tradition (see Part Six), the Gray Man would be considered a spirit that wants to do good but is trapped in a between-worlds pattern, destined to repeat the same behavior over and over. He may have entered the next world and then, somehow, returned to this one—perhaps to a place he loved, to protect people he loved. He continues to walk quietly along Pawley's Island until the next time danger threatens someone there.

Pawley's Island is a barrier island, or a scrap of sandy land, north of Charleston. It is a little less than four miles long and about a quarter mile wide, a place where residents like to say nothing changes and nobody hurries. It would have been a popular retreat for some Charleston plantation owners who built summer homes on the island because it was breezy, less humid, and there were fewer mosquitoes than on their plantations. For them, it would have been a vacation spot, and to some degree it still is. In the year 2000 just 138 people lived on the island full-time. Another community on the inland side of the causeway, also called Pawley's Island, is a commercially developed area with a different ambience and, as far as anybody has reported, is not home to any ghosts at all.

The most popular account of the Gray Man's legend is a love story. A young, engaged woman and her family were staying on Pawley's Island sometime early in the 1800s. They were expecting her fiancé, who had been away for several months, to join them and had been busy preparing his favorite foods for his welcome. They were looking forward to his arrival, and he was just as eager to get there.

When he got to the island, he was in such a hurry to see his betrothed again that he left the main path and took a shortcut, riding his horse through a marsh without really inspecting it first. That turned out to be a mistake. Quicksand in the area, not immediately obvious, sucked the horse and the young man down so deeply that they could not struggle out. The harder they fought, the faster the sand pulled them down, deeper and deeper. The horse died. So did its rider.

Nobody knows for sure how the news of this tragedy reached his fiancée and her family, but according to a classic version of the story, a servant who had been riding with him saw the whole thing but was powerless to help. Eventually he, or somebody, brought the terrible news to the waiting girl and her family.

The girl was disconsolate. Theirs had been a true love match, not a marriage arranged for social prestige or family convenience. After her love's death, she walked the beach every day, often for hours at a time, grieving. One morning, she saw the figure of a man in gray clothing, and even though his features were vague, she knew it was her dead fiancé. He warned her that she and her family must get off the island at once because a bad storm was coming. Did he actually speak, or did she understand his message intuitively? They had always enjoyed a knack for knowing one another's thoughts without talking much.

The man disappeared as suddenly as he had come, and the young woman ran to the house to tell her parents about her experience. What happened next depends on who tells the story. In one version, they all took the warning to heart and fled to the mainland without taking the time to collect any belongings. Soon afterward, the hurricane hit the mainland with force and also roared across the island, destroying everything in its path. Seeing the devastation everywhere when they returned to the island, the girl and her family were astonished to find their own home unharmed.

In another retelling, the young woman's family began worrying about her extreme mourning. She told them that she had seen her fiancé on the beach, but when she moved toward him, he was washed away by a wave. Another time, she dreamed of floating in a tiny boat tossed by waves while her fiancé waved to her from shore, trying to urge her in. When she told her family about that dream, her father decided they needed professional help. He took the whole family to Charleston to consult a doctor. While they were gone, a storm hit the area, killing many people. In this version, the young woman realized when they returned that her fiancé had come back to the island to keep her safe. Feeling loved even though she could not see him, she gave up mourning and went on to lead a happy life. But she never married because she was committed to the Gray Man.

From that time on, the Gray Man's appearances came to be considered as warnings to leave the island because of an approaching storm. At least two sightings were reported in the 1800s, one before the hurricane of 1822 that hit the Charleston area and resulted in more than three hundred deaths on the islands. The details about that sighting are vague, and there may have been others that never made it into popular legend at all. Then in 1893, the Lachicotte family saw the Gray Man and, having heard stories about his warnings, left the island, escaping the Sea Islands Hurricane that killed as many as fifteen hundred people.

By 1954 weather forecasting was becoming more accurate but still could not always predict exact times and places for heavy storms, so people continued to take the Gray Man's appearances seriously. A woman vacationing on the island with her children and grandchildren saw a man in gray appear on the beach and then fade away as she watched. Another time, someone, possibly one of the grandchildren, tried to chase the apparition. It disappeared at once. The next day, tornados, which are hard to predict even today, hit the area. Though we don't know if the family left the island in time or not, they must have lived to tell the tale.

That was also the year of Hurricane Hazel. With winds blowing from 125 to 150 miles per hour, the October storm destroyed buildings along the coast and on the island. At least nineteen people died. Bill Collins and his bride might have been among them if it weren't for the Gray Man. They were on their honeymoon and had not paid much attention to the weather. They were not listening to a radio, nor did they have access to a television, so they were puzzled when someone knocked at their door very early in the morning. When Bill answered the door, he saw a man dressed in rumpled gray pants and a gray shirt. The man told them that the Red Cross had sent him to warn people that a storm was coming and to ask them to leave the island. We don't know whether he spoke, since he usually didn't, or was able to communicate the message silently. Either way, after that he simply disappeared. Too shaken to question the experience, the couple got off the island just hours before Hurricane Hazel blew in, a Category 4 storm that killed ninety-five people and destroyed fifteen thousand homes. Other island residents later said they had seen a lone man in gray clothing walking on the beach before the storm came in. If those residents didn't evacuate, they must have found a safe haven because they lived to talk about the experience later.

By 1989, the year of Hurricane Hugo, weather forecasting was becoming increasingly precise, so people knew that the hurricane was coming, though they could not have imagined the damage it would do. The storm was so strong that it blew inland as far as Charlotte, North Carolina, at 94 miles per hour, taking out many of the trees that had earned the place the name "Shady City." Nobody on the coast could have imagined it. At the same time, the legend of Gray Man had become well known and respected by many on the island, who interpreted his presence as a warning of danger. One couple, permanent residents, saw the Gray Man as they were walking on the beach on September 19. They waved casually, in the Southern way, as he came toward them. He disappeared. They took his presence seriously and left the island right away, long before Hugo blew in.

Hugo turned out to be the biggest natural disaster South Carolina had ever known, although even weather forecasters could not have predicted that ahead of time. By Thursday, October 21, Governor Carroll Campbell had ordered evacuation of the island. One couple, who left before the storm hit, endured frightening hours inland at McClellan-ville, a small town between Charleston and Pawley's Island. There a high school gymnasium nearly twenty feet above sea level, which had been built specifically to withstand high winds, was opened as a storm refuge. The building was okay against the wind, but nobody had expected the great tidal surge that filled the gym with so much water people began swimming out the windows. Nobody died there, but nobody ever forgot the experience, either.

If the storm was terrifying, its aftermath was devastating in the randomness of destruction. Flooding could wash away an entire house yet leave behind a coffeepot sitting on a stove in an otherwise empty area. One might look up and see a child's red wagon wedged high in the branches of a tree.

Given all that they saw on the mainland, when the couple who had seen the Gray Man returned to their island four days later, they expected the worst. They were right. Homes were just gone. Sometimes the top half of a home sat on its lot, while the bottom floor was two blocks away. Pieces of who-knew-what littered the area, so the returning couple was prepared for their loss as they drove to their own house, or, they figured, to the spot where it once had stood. What they saw probably came as a greater shock than finding their home gone: The place was untouched, perfectly intact. Nothing was jarred, jiggled, or moved, inside or out. Their story made the local news.

Since then, Gray Man stories persist, often related by an island resident to a shopkeeper on the mainland, told to a visiting journalist, or repeated on TV shows such as *Unsolved Mysteries*. In all these accounts, the Gray Man is recognizable and benevolent, but occasionally another version surfaces. In that one he is a malevolent spirit, the ghost of Edward Teach—otherwise known as Blackbeard the pirate.

Blackbeard did sail and plunder up and down this coastal area, but everyone knows that his head was cut off in a shipboard battle, and after he was thrown overboard in a North Carolina inlet, he swam around the ship seven times before he sank. The Gray Man hasn't done any plundering that anybody has reported, and his apparition has its head, wearing a hat, firmly attached. According to another report, though, when several people walking together on the beach at sunset saw him floating near the edge of the water, he didn't appear to have any legs. Perhaps the evening fog was just moving in?

Scholar and author Charles Joyner, formerly a Southern history professor at Coastal Carolina University, knows Pawley's Island well and has stayed at the Pelican Inn, where owners and guests have sometimes reported seeing the spirit. He says that the Gray Man legend seems to have evolved through media stories and personal accounts rather than as a legend in folklore, told to groups around a flickering flame. But he also acknowledges that today's media— TV, the Internet, and YouTube—have changed the nature of popular legend, so stories may persist electronically without the print or face-to-face communication that once developed a legend.

When Joyner was in the area to record interviews with the children and grandchildren of slaves, he had a room at the Pelican, where some people have reported seeing the Gray Man. Joyner kept his tape recorder at the ready, just in case the spirit of the Gray Man wanted to be in touch. Alas, no contact.

But as the weather has become increasingly aberrant in recent years, folks who live on Pawley's Island still watch out for the Gray Man. With all due respect for sophisticated weather forecasting, the forecasters are doing a job. The Gray Man *cares*. One wonders why he would stay around now that his lady love is long gone? Perhaps he has no place else to go and will spend his eternity walking quietly on the island, doing what he can to protect the people who live on this place he still loves.

Chapter 17

The Silent Scream

Aiken-Rhett House
48 Elizabeth Street

The Aiken-Rhett House was one of the most opulent homes in Charleston, the site of many grand parties for important and wealthy people. It was built in 1820. South Carolina Governor William Aiken Jr. and his wife, Harriet, remodeled the house and enlarged it sometime around 1839. The Aikens kept a staff of seven hundred slaves to work their rice plantation, with about a dozen in town to maintain the property on Elizabeth Street and serve family and guests. The Aiken-Rhett House is owned and maintained now by the Historic Charleston Foundation and is open daily for tours. Some visitors see the unhappy people who never recovered from the loss of the old way of life.

Judy hadn't come to Charleston for ghosts. She'd come to study the city's historic preservation sites, hoping to develop ideas to apply to her own community's preservation efforts in North Carolina. Well, okay, she had to admit that she was also there for the food. Who wouldn't be? The Aiken-Rhett House stands as an outstanding example of preservation versus renovation. Although the building is carefully maintained, it has changed little since 1858.

Judy was the first tourist to be admitted to the Aiken-Rhett House at 10:00 a.m. one Monday morning. She followed the tape-recorded tour guide and marveled at how much there was to see.

Judy knew the story told by Ed Macy and Julian Buxton III about the experiences of two architects who were in the building after dark in 1989. They had worked much of the summer measuring and describing the building in detail to create an official record for the Historical American Building Survey and had returned only to check the mansion's monitoring system. As one last chore before they quit, the two men headed to the second floor to close the windows in the ballroom because the security monitors had detected wind blowing in.

When they hit the stairs, they were stopped by an ear-piercing noise that got painfully louder as they went up. It seemed to be coming from the ballroom, where the door was rattling noisily. Some of us might have turned tail and hustled back down the stairs, because it was late and dark. But the architects did not. They were young men, there were two of them, and they had flashlights. When they touched the door, the noise stopped, and inside the ballroom all was as it should have been—windows closed, no wind at all. They walked around the ballroom, using their flashlights just to make sure everything was okay.

Everything looked normal until they saw something moving reflected in the mirror. They heard sobbing that seemed to go on and on. Then they saw the image of an old woman in the mirror. She had long, white hair that blew about as if the wind they'd heard earlier was pummeling her, and her face was awful in its anguish. Her mouth was open wide and her eyes were staring straight ahead. She put her hands against her cheeks and wailed until she quivered. That's what the men saw, but they did not hear anything at all. Her scream, like the wind now, was silent.

It was one of those old stories that had passed among architects for a while, but Judy didn't take it seriously. She was an architect too, and she thought some of those young guys would have been capable of amusing themselves with a story like that. She was entirely neutral on the whole notion of ghosts existing—maybe, maybe not. Besides, all that had happened in 1989, and it was now 2011. Ownership of the house had passed from the Charleston Museum to the Historic Charleston Foundation. She had heard that visitors sometimes heard unexplained sounds or saw the pale form of a woman drifting about, but she didn't take any of it seriously. She was there for the architecture.

The three-story house has four rooms on each floor, with piazzas and fences of cypress and cedar, while there are spacious cellars and storerooms beneath the house. These are maintained but not "improved" in any way, and many of the furnishings the Aikens brought back from Europe are still in their original places. No electricity has ever been added to the house except in the basement. Slave quarters, also preserved, stand behind the main house. Although they were stark and spare, they apparently were sound and livable and show signs of having been painted bright colors, including the "haint blue" seen throughout Charleston. The stable, carriage house, kitchen, and laundry were all behind the house, with the slaves' dormitory above the kitchen and stable. And, perhaps for appearances' sake, these buildings were fronted with Gothic Revival facades that didn't add to the buildings' functionality but helped everything on the property look of a piece.

It would be hard to overstate the opulence of the good years (from the Aikens' point of view). Slaves working in the main house included household servants, a butler, maids, nurses, chambermaids, and cooks. Those of lesser rank were carriage drivers, gardeners, carpenters, and stablemen. The kitchen was an outside building, as in most mansions back then, but in the basement of the mansion was a "warming kitchen" space dedicated to arranging prepared foods on serving platters, garnishing them, and keeping them at proper temperature until serving time. Those slaves who worked in the house would have been highly trained and dressed in uniforms appropriate for serving important guests. After one visit there, Jefferson Davis referred to the slaves' "noiseless automatic service . . . where your own servants think for you."

The Aikens remodeled the house extensively when they owned it, making it complement their social standing and entertaining habits. The later decision to preserve the building rather than renovate it was especially important because, unlike most of the mansions and other buildings on the city's south side, this one escaped serious damage from the Federals' bombardment and fires. The great fire of 1861 had already destroyed much of the northern part of Charleston. The Aiken-Rhett House represented one opportunity to show all who cared what the past had looked like for the wealthy and influential Charleston citizens.

After Governor Aiken and Harriet died, their daughter, Henrietta Rhett, and her husband inherited the house, making it the Aiken-Rhett House instead of simply the Aiken House. They, in turn, left it to their children. One of the Rhett sons bought it from the others in 1949 and lived there with his wife. After he died, his widow donated it to the Charleston Museum in 1975.

In 1995 the Historic Charleston Foundation bought the house. The foundation continues to operate it as a museum, open daily. Most visitors take the tape-recorded tour, stopping to examine points of interest to them, but every so often someone reports seeing a shadowy figure walk through the downstairs hall. And when not wearing headphones to listen to the tour tape, a tourist will sometimes hear odd noises in what appear to be empty rooms. Could they be signs of Harriet's unwillingness to give up the good life? We can only guess at how she felt as the ease and glamor she'd once known disappeared. Socially, it was the end of an era.

After her husband died, she turned the grand ballroom into a large bedroom for herself and lived mostly in that room. Upon her death, her daughter simply locked the ballroom door, and the room remained closed off until 1975, when the Charleston Museum took over. This was good news for preservationists, but what about the spirits that remembered better times?

✛

Although she admired what remained of the fine old art and furnishings, Judy did not give much thought to the notion that family spirits remained in the house. Then, in the east drawing room, she came upon the portrait of Harriet Aiken, painted in her glory days as the wife of Governor William Aiken Jr. It was a larger-than-life depiction, showing a beautiful woman in a tasteful but impressive off-the-shoulder gown with a lacy overlay, softly cinched at the waist, sweeping the floor. Harriet's long, dark hair was parted down the middle and drawn loosely back over her ears with a feather ornament in the back. She looked wealthy, confident, almost stern.

Judy stopped at the painting for a long time. In addition to architecture, her passions included textiles and clothing. This gown was something she might never see elsewhere. She knew photography was not allowed in the museum, so she made some sketches. This took a while.

When Judy looked up one more time as she was finishing, the woman in the portrait was staring directly at her. Judy was unnerved. Something in the portrait was trying to tell her something, and it did not feel to Judy like it was anything pleasant. One doesn't have to believe in ghosts to know when a woman is staring down at her. Judy definitely did not want to engage. Besides, it was almost lunchtime, which suited her just fine. She hightailed it out of the museum in search of a good Charleston meal. She did not know where she wanted to go—except, for sure, not Poogan's Porch (see page 34), where people see an old woman in the mirror watching them. She did not want any more dead women looking at her.

Judy's focus had been on the museum's interior, but other people have reported strange sightings and even photographed some outside the building. Two entries on the Grave Addiction website (www.graveaddiction.com) mention other oddities seen but not heard here. In June 2006 J. R. Davis posted a note about a face he thought he'd identified in the remnants of paint on an exterior wall of the slave quarters. He circled it on the digital photo. A little later he posted a second note, saying he'd found two more faces, which he circled, making three in all—one large and two smaller. Of course this is a reminder that the slaves who lived and worked on the property lost a secure way of life after the Civil War, and some of them, probably devoted to the Aiken family, might check on the old place from time to time. On the other hand, because slavery definitely had its cruelty, some spirits may have left marks to express their anger about how they had been treated in the past.

A man named John Ferguson took photographs outside looking into the mansion just before going inside for a wedding reception. One photo shows an ornately decorated room, another a second-floor balcony with a window behind it. Something unidentified fills a corner of the window in each photo. Ferguson says his pictures show a male figure in a three-cornered hat at the window, though nobody who was there at the time saw this man. Ferguson felt sure that what he'd seen wasn't a regular guest, because the apparition was in period costume and this was a wedding reception, not a costume ball.

But looking at Harriet Aiken's larger-than-life color portrait and having her look back may be the most eerie experience of all for some visitors, if they are not used to it.

An older Charleston woman who volunteers once a week at the Aiken-Rhett House said, "I've known this house all my life, and I've never seen a ghost." But she admits that Harriet looks directly at her from within that huge, elaborate frame on the wall. What does the volunteer do when she sees that? "Why, I just smile and say, 'Hello.'"

Chapter 18
Theatrical Spirits

Dock Street Theatre
135 Church Street

The Dock Street Theatre is a state-of-the-art performance venue with a complicated history, said to be haunted by more than one ghost. The theater was built in 1735 and burned down just four years later in a fire that destroyed much of Charleston. The structure was rebuilt as a glamorous hotel that later declined, and the building became a theater again during the Great Depression. In 2010, after another renovation, the building reopened as an up-to-date theater seating about 450 people. The ghost of an actor who sometimes stayed at the inn has been reported there. So has that of Nettie Dickerson, once favored as a lady of the night by some wealthy Planters Hotel guests. Other spirits that nobody can identify show up frequently, including noisy children who are heard but not seen and a man with no visible legs who moves silently.

During the 2007–2010 renovation of the Dock Street Theatre, funded by the city of Charleston, Isiah Nesbitt, nick-named Rabbit, worked for NBM Construction Company on the project. He unlocked the doors each morning and closed the place up at night. Every morning he saw a young woman at the top of the stairs—or, to be exact, he saw her down to her knees, which seemed to disappear into the floor. And he said he sometimes he heard an angry man growling on the stage. Rabbit wasn't scared because he'd seen lots of ghosts while working on big renovation projects around Charleston. "I see ghosts all the time," he said.

On the other hand, the master carpenter and stagehand Randy Jones, who is not a timid man, had such an unnerving experience in the theater at the end of a performance of *The Legend of Sleepy Hollow* that he told the story on YouTube (www.youtube.com/watch?v=4CiwwNE-gl4). Randy, who had ten years' experience, didn't worry much about staying to close up the building after all the audience and performers had left. He did it all the time. The night he heard heavy footsteps clomping in the hall on the second floor, Randy figured it was Seth, a red-haired actor who performed as Ichabod Crane and was usually the last one out. Randy went upstairs to lock the door after Seth left, but when he got to the hallway, he saw nobody, although he could still hear the heavy steps that sounded like Seth's. He called out to Seth. No response. An invisible something, stomping around in big boots—just not normal. Randy skittered away from the hall, slammed the door, and reached behind himself to lock it without looking back. Now Randy says that the theater is "a scary place at night."

Another backstage worker says he hears children whispering and giggling in the balcony, sometimes before shows begin, although he never sees them. He also catches sight of a man he can't see from the waist down moving somewhere in the balcony. This stagehand tends to stand behind a curtain or post to hide from these visions, a little like the kid's notion, "If I can't see you, you can't see me."

Some audience members claim to have seen a beautiful woman in a red dress on the theater's balcony and in the second-floor hallway. And a local woman snapped a picture of the balcony from outside late at night that shows a figure she believes must be a ghost. She's never been able to duplicate that shot, even when she's invited the apparition to show itself again.

You have to wonder how resident ghosts can still find their way to the Dock Street Theatre after it's been through so many changes. Not only did the property shift from theater to prestigious inn to Works Progress Administration-restored theater to the state-of-the-art performance center funded by the City of Charleston, at various times the place also served as a cheap hotel, a food store, and a second-hand shop. Moreover, the street it's on is now called Church Street; the name "Dock Street" disappeared along with the dock on the creek some time ago.

Even for Charleston, this place saw an unusual number of revivals and declines. After the fire of 1735, the theater was rebuilt, later fell into wreckage, and was replaced in the 1800s by the elaborate and famous Planters Inn. Still later, an earthquake and the Civil War reduced that to shambles. It wasn't until the 1930s that the Works Progress Administration (WPA) restored the building, once again as a theater. In 2007 the City of Charleston began yet another renovation that took nearly three years. Each rebuilding and renovation incorporated the sites of other buildings that had been adjacent to the original theater, creating new spaces, adding and knocking down walls, changing ceiling heights. If you imagine the process as a sped-up film clip, it's as though structures were built, allowed to deteriorate, and rebuilt, repeatedly, with old materials flying away from the site and new ones replacing them.

For instance, when the Planters Inn hotel replaced the theater in 1809, it meant adding guest rooms, dining rooms, a kitchen, and public areas. Then in 1835, an elaborate wrought-iron balcony was added to the hotel. This balcony, which has remained a constant on the building ever since, is reputed to be the most photographed structure in Charleston. It's painted "haint blue," a color that is supposed to keep ghosts away. Apparently that hasn't worked here. The 1930s WPA project that restored the building as a theater raised the second-story floors more than a foot and created a pit for common people, a higher gallery for women, and balcony boxes for wealthy citizens. Modern renovations funded by the City of Charleston, finished in 2010, added sound and light equipment suited for music and plays and an auditorium seating about 450 people. You would think all those changes, from dining rooms to stages with thrift shops in between, would be enough to confuse ghosts, but they keep showing up.

Maybe it's that wrought-iron balcony added while the Planters Hotel still operated in its prime that works as a marker. The lady in red—the ghost of Nettie Dickerson, a beautiful prostitute—can always find it. When the Planters Hotel was a bawdy, prestigious place frequented by travelers and the wealthy men of Charleston, Nettie's beauty and lively personality allowed her to earn plenty of money as a lady of the night. She wore gorgeous clothes, including a daringly low-cut, silky red dress.

But Nellie had not intended to become a prostitute. When she came to Charleston to escape a dull life as a country girl in upstate South Carolina, she thought her job at the prestigious St. Philip's Episcopal Church, where she met members of Charleston's elite society, would win her entry into it. She ran errands for the priests and arranged social events for the church. She was smart, and people liked her—in her place. It didn't matter how charming she was or how lovely, the elite of antebellum Charleston weren't inclined to accept her as their own. She didn't come from a wealthy, important family. But that didn't stop men from inviting her to join them in illicit relationships while they remained safely married.

Eventually frustration, or fury, drove her to use her looks and charm as a prostitute and to flaunt it around sedate wives. Also, at this point she may have come to realize what historians and old diaries document: The men of Charleston society indulged in all kinds of hedonistic pleasures. They belonged to clubs and had different places to go for fun virtually every night of the week. They engaged openly in encounters with available women, including the enslaved Africans, and didn't hesitate to talk about it.

Nettie must have begun understanding all this, working in the church and observing its wellborn families as she settled in. When men began inviting her to become their mistress, perhaps she saw the one way she could gain a kind of equality, even though no woman of society would approve.

As she became popular and increasingly flamboyant in her role as "escort," Nettie found, not surprisingly, that she wasn't welcomed in St. Philip's Episcopal Church as a member anymore. But the church still figured in her life. Often she would stand on the balcony of the Planters Hotel looking out at the church's spire.

One night as she stood on the balcony, gripping the metal rail, a raging storm moved in, with the wind, thunder, and lightning typical of the coast. But Nettie didn't go inside. The storm, whipping her hair and drenching her, was too exciting. And, just like that, it was over for Nettie. It took only a single bolt of lightning, attracted to the elaborate ironwork of the balcony, to kill her before she even had time to think about death, let alone prepare for it.

Some people say she still doesn't know she's dead. Others believe she just isn't willing to leave a life that, however questionable its morals, was exciting. Now she wanders the halls and balcony of the theater that was once the Planters Inn, walking through walls and ignoring floors that are higher than they were when the building was still a hotel.

Apparently, Nettie's ghost never meets the male ghost of Junius Brutus Booth, father of John Wilkes Booth, the actor who assassinated President Lincoln. Junius was an actor too. He and his theatrical troupe stayed at the Planters Inn when they were performing at the New Theatre in Charleston. In those years, actors could be a pretty rowdy gang, and according to local legend, Junius tried to kill his manager in 1838. He wasn't successful, but the story suggests that a murderous impulse ran in the Booth family.

Nobody seems to know why Junius hangs around, but they say that, like Nettie, he walks through walls and seems unaware that floors have been raised since the old hotel days. Some folks speculate that Junius liked the Planters Hotel so much he just didn't want to leave—ever. But you have to wonder what would've kept him around during that building's low-rent years before the end of the Civil War. Or could the theory of some paranormal investigators be true, that a ghost from one era may open the way for ghosts from other times?

Not everybody actually sees Junius. Some, like stagehand Randy Jones, just hear an invisible person stomping around. That's plenty for Randy.

These days the theater hosts Spoleto Festival USA each year, and the resident professional theater, Charleston Stage, produces more than 120 performances a year. The theater is definitely a jewel in Charleston's crown, but it's probably not a venue where it's a good idea to wish performers good luck with the theater standard, "break a leg."

Part Five

PLANTATION HAUNTS

It is hard to imagine a plantation with no spirits around. These places, on the islands around the city of Charleston, have long, complicated histories. Many stories involve Southern gentlemen trying to grow crops with which they were not familiar; slaves who kept the fields and household going; a good bit of Gullah influence, often a mixture of Christianity, old African beliefs, and traditions; and, undeniably, violence.

Chapter 19
Ghosties and Ghostly Lovers

Fenwick Hall Plantation

George Fenwick was the first Fenwick from England to arrive at John's Island, off the coast of Charleston. It was 1694. His ship, Loyal Jamaica, was a pirate vessel. George decided to abandon his life of piracy and settle in the area. In 1704 his brother John also came to the island, and by 1730 he had made enough money to build Fenwick Hall, a beautiful, brick Georgian-style plantation house. By the time John's son, Edward Fenwick, had inherited the property, there was more than enough money to allow for an expansion of that house. His family lived graciously here. But the Fenwick men had a history of violence, so it's no surprise that several ghosts have haunted the place over the years.

When you see the photographs and learn the history of Fenwick Hall Plantation on John's Island in Charleston County, you can almost believe that the place was deliberately designed to be haunted. It is now private property, and the owners will prosecute trespassers, but thanks to a lifelong project begun by John R. Hauser when he was ten years old, you can see photos of the house and grounds as they changed over time and read detailed accounts of plantation history (www.fenwickhall.com). The house was full of secrets—hidden stairs and doors, and even a hidden tunnel that ran from the basement to the Stono River.

What were all the hidey-holes for? Perhaps when George Fenwick gave up piracy, he kept his treasure and needed a place to hide it. Maybe he didn't even trust some of the men who had been fellow privateers. Then, later, important military men from the Revolutionary War to the Civil War spent time on the island, making the Fenwicks, who were said to change loyalties from time to time, feel the need for escape routes in the event that armed men threatened them.

However, in its heyday, no such worries on the plantation were obvious. The grounds of the property, more than a thousand acres, were beautifully landscaped, with flower gardens, magnolias, and huge, old live oak trees whose horizontal branches dripped with greenish gray-white strands of Spanish moss. Hanging Spanish moss looks ghostly even without old stories to fire the imagination. The plantation's main crop was Sea Island cotton, which required slaves to work all over the island as well as in the house, so slaves probably knew some of those hidden places both in the house and around the island.

For Edward Fenwick, cotton was just a crop, though a highly profitable one. He had a different passion: thoroughbred racehorses and racing. He made money at that too. He is credited with establishing turf grass in the Carolinas and with importing the best horses available from England, to race, breed, and sell. Thanks in part to his efforts, racing became a popular sport in Charleston.

Edward's teenage daughter, Ann, loved horses as much as he did. This formed a strong bond between them. Although Edward was known to be harsh in his business dealings, he doted on Ann, with whom he was always kind and generous. When she was seventeen, he imported a magnificent black racer from England as a special present for her. Of course, knowing how to handle horses, she was so thrilled that she rode every day, always with the company of one of the grooms. As the daughter of a wealthy plantation owner, Ann could ride and leave the more physical care of her horse to the grooms.

Horses are all different; so are grooms. And that's where the trouble started. Ann saw that one of them, Tony, had a special, gentle way with her animal, and she liked that. Being a seventeen-year-old girl, she also saw that Tony was good-looking, well mannered, articulate, and sweet. Soon she began to ask specifically to have Tony accompany her as she rode.

Perhaps it was inevitable; two comely young people with common interests spending long periods of time alone together were bound to develop a strong attraction for one another. Soon they wanted to be married. Seventeen was not too young for a girl to wed back then, so Ann decided to ask her father for permission to marry Tony. At the time, daughters couldn't make any major choices without the approval of a father or guardian. But because her father had always been so indulgent with her, Ann did not really expect much trouble with this request. She knew that Tony had come from a family of gentility and that he was determined to make his way independently in a new country. He was a groom, but he was also a gentleman. And she loved him.

Edward Fenwick's response wasn't at all what she expected. "Absolutely not," he said. "The daughter of a plantation owner does not marry a common stable hand."

She tried to explain Tony's background, but Fenwick wouldn't listen. "Absolutely not" was his final decision. Some time later, when she tried to repeat the request, he simply told her not to mention it again. No meant no.

Ann and Tony decided that if they couldn't marry with her father's blessing, they'd just elope without his approval, then start new lives in Charles Town proper. In a village beyond the plantation, near the Ashley River, they found a minister who pronounced them man and wife without question, but afterward it turned out to be too late to find transport across the river until morning. They were in a romantic mood, not frightened, and spent the night happily enough in a deserted cabin. Just as the sun came up, they heard a terrible commotion—shouting and the rattling of a carriage outside the cabin—and before they'd had time to react, the door burst open, and angry men seized Tony while an even angrier father forced Ann into the carriage. The whole group headed back to the plantation.

Faster than Ann could grasp what was happening, the men had a noose around Tony's neck, set him on a horse, tied the other end of the rope to one of the long branches of a live oak tree, and whipped the horse out from under him. Ann fainted dead away. The horse lurched out from under Tony with such speed that, as he was hung, the noose severed his head from his body.

Ann was never the same again. Her mind rejected the reality of what had happened, and she wandered around the house and plantation, looking for Tony. She never rode another horse, and she never left the plantation. And after she died, her spirit still would not leave. She continued to look for Tony.

As for Tony, even if he understood what had happened, he never accepted it either and was sometimes seen on bright nights, headless, riding a horse. Was he looking for his head or for Ann—or, perhaps, for both?

As dramatic as this story is, it's not the only spooky tale to arise on the island. Every so often, someone sees a group of Confederate soldiers marching along a live oak-lined side road on the island, pale but recognizable as soldiers in uniform. So far, nobody has figured out why the soldiers have remained long after their deaths, whether from natural causes or military trauma. It is possible that they are caught in a loop, repeating a single traumatic event over and over, and cannot escape into the next world.

Let's not forget about the ghosties, either, though their presence does not suggest such violence. The Fenwick Hall website thanks John Swanger for his recollection of spooky events in Fenwick Hall, as his Aunt Annie told him about her youthful days visiting Aunt Nelly and Uncle Clauds there. After the children went to bed at night, they heard a lot of crashing around downstairs, but they never saw anything moving when they sneaked down to see what was happening. The next morning, though, all the furniture would have been moved into new places. At first they'd move it all back where it belonged, but the same thing would happen all over again, night after night. In the end, Aunt Nelly, who called the beings "ghosties," just left the furniture wherever she found it, saying, "Well, they live here too."

Today Fenwick Plantation has shrunk to just a little more than fifty acres. The house, Fenwick Hall, has fallen to near-ruin and has been rescued more than once. During the Civil War, the building served as a hospital for Confederate and Union soldiers. In the 1980s it became a hospital for treating drug and alcohol addiction and maintained that status until it closed in 1995. In each of these periods, changes were made inside the house, adding to its mystery. Current restoration efforts have focused on removing such earlier additions as a hospital kitchen and returning the building to its original state. The larger plantation, though, has been taken over by real estate development, leaving Fenwick Hall on its fifty-five acres surrounded by new development. What will happen to Fenwick's ghosts? Will they continue to appear in the shrunken acreage of the plantation, move into the new homes being built on the island, or disappear for good?

Chapter 20
The Heartbroken Ghost

Hampton Plantation
950 Rutledge Road, McClellanville

Hampton Plantation had a prestigious and prosperous history before becoming a state historic site, but one heir, John Henry Rutledge, came to a sad end with a broken heart, and is still heard banging around the mansion.

Some of the tour interpreters at Hampton Plantation find what they see and hear so frightening that they refuse to stay there after dark. Enough people have reported seeing a male ghost on the stairs and hearing unexplained sounds to attract the attention of paranormal investigators, who try to record what they call electronic voice phenomena. One recording, submitted by "Joelie" to the website angelsghosts.com, contains what Joelie believes is a man's voice saying, "I'm mad."

What he might be mad about is not being able to marry the love of his life because his family was too socially and financially prominent. True love didn't seem to stand much of a chance among young people in the era of huge plantations and huge profits, for these carried with them the obligation to maintain high social status by marrying well. This meant the "right" person with upper class credentials. Lots of marriages took place without the notion of love being considered. That was the price of prestige.

To say that Hampton Plantation had been a prestigious place is an understatement. Daniel Horry began the rice plantation in 1744. As the years passed, the list of well-known people who lived there grew. These names still command respect in South Carolina today: Huger, Horry, Pinckney, Middleton, Rutledge. They formed a long chain of important people whose offspring married well.

But some of the heirs apparent at Hampton Plantation apparently did not want anything to do with it. The place and its people survived the Revolutionary War, British presence at the plantation, and the Civil War. After that, indifference threatened the place for a while. Daniel Horry, the son of Daniel Huger Horry, inherited the estate when his father died in 1785, but instead of taking over, he changed his name and moved to Europe, leaving his mother and grandmother to run the property. Near the end of the eighteenth century, Harriott Horry Rutledge moved to the plantation with her husband, Frederick. Eventually she inherited it. Her grandson, Henry Middleton Rutledge, managed the plantation and later married Margaret Hamilton Seabrook. Their son, Archibald, left to become a professor of English in Pennsylvania but eventually came back to Hampton Plantation in 1937 after having lived as he chose, away from family obligations.

John Henry Rutledge, one of the sons of Harriott and Frederick Rutledge, didn't get off so easily. He didn't run away to Europe or even Pennsylvania; he stayed with the family on the plantation. He was just twenty-one when he met the daughter of a pharmacist in Georgetown and fell in love. His parents were horrified when he spoke of marrying her. His mother, Harriott Horry Rutledge, told him that a pharmacist could be useful if one needed medicine, but the position held no social prestige at all. A pharmacist's daughter was not an appropriate match because it would bring no social benefits to the family or the plantation. A pharmacist's daughter certainly wouldn't be qualified to carry out the social niceties required for the mistress of the place. She would not know the fine points of arranging seating for dinners in the mansion, how to manage a guest-invitation list, or what kinds of dresses to wear for various occasions. She surely would not understand the rules of making and receiving social calls.

We don't know if Harriott actually said it or not, but at the time in Charleston, some other people of the Rutledges' class would have looked down on a family whose son married beneath his status. It just wasn't done if you valued your place in society. Nobody but John Henry was talking about love at all. Still, he didn't give up. Defying his parents, he went to the pharmacy to talk to his love's father. He asked for permission to marry her, which was standard practice in those days for a young man. This father said "no."

John Henry did not give up and soon returned to plead his case again, emphasizing how well off a young woman marrying into his family would be. One might assume that a man would be happy to see his daughter marry "up," but it didn't work that way. The pharmacist said he understood the class system as it had come from England, and while they could be perfectly cordial in professional relationships, as they usually were, he knew that the Rutledge family would always look down on his daughter if she married John Henry. She may have come to the same conclusion, because she married someone else soon thereafter, leaving John Henry with a broken heart. He must have wondered too, given how soon she moved on, if she ever had cared about him as much as he had about her.

After that, John Henry moped and mourned, spending most of his time in a rocking chair by the window of his room overlooking the garden. Sometimes he went downstairs to the library. He seemed to like it there. Others in the family laughed at him and told him to snap out of his misery. The world was full of charming young ladies who would be thrilled to be with him.

He just got more depressed. His mother arranged visits from families with marriageable daughters who were perfectly pleasant and pretty, but if he met them at all, he sat passively, not even trying to sustain polite conversation. His sisters invited their most charming friends to visit, hoping he would find one of them appealing. They invited him to take jaunts into Charleston to go to the theater or visit other families with them, but he always refused and just rocked in his chair as he watched them leave.

His mother and sisters arranged an especially fine party in the mansion's ballroom, where there would be music and dancing and good food and spirits. They coaxed him to come: "Everybody will be there. You might have a good time."

Party night turned out to be rainy, and John Henry wouldn't go. He probably would have refused no matter what the weather, but the rain outside plus the gaiety he didn't share inside made him more miserable than ever. He sat in his room and rocked and moped.

Later, he went to the library and took out a gun he'd hidden there, went to the top of the stairs, and shot himself in the head. He fell to the bottom of the steps, where he was found in a puddle of blood. He didn't die until two days later.

No one knows whether anyone in the family sought medications that might have helped him from the pharmacy. But in that time while he lingered, old stories have it that he forgave his family for keeping him from the woman he loved and also asked their forgiveness for bringing scandal to the plantation. At the time, people believed suicide victims could not be buried in sacred ground, so the family buried John Henry in the garden, not a cemetery. As the legend has it, his body may have been buried, but something about him remained aboveground. The most notable sign was that his chair rocked by itself when nobody was in it. This persisted until the day the chair was taken from the house. Even now, some people hear the rocking sound although they see no chair. A daughter of freed slaves who lived on the plantation said that the bloodstain on the floor where he fell could never be removed, no matter how hard they scrubbed.

South Carolina poet laureate and author Archibald Rutledge, the one who moved to Pennsylvania to pursue a literary life and live free of the plantation before returning "home," died in 1973. Before he died, he willed the plantation, which he had inherited, to the state of South Carolina. The state maintains it now as a historic site. Some visitors and tour guides say that even today they see and hear unexplained activity in the mansion. Lights turn on by themselves, and odd noises come from various places in the building—especially from the library, where John Henry might still be moping or, perhaps, looking for his hidden gun.

Some contemporary ghost hunters have claimed to see him on the stairs, which would make sense if he was reliving the moment of retrieving the gun in the library and taking it back upstairs to kill himself.

Visitors also claim to hear a chair rocking in the library, even though the chair is gone and had always been upstairs in John Henry's room. But sound tends to carry through floors in old houses, even the grand ones. Perhaps this is a phantom memory of sound John Henry's family would have heard when they were downstairs and he was up in his room rocking away.

Other visitors have been less specific, neither hearing nor seeing anything in particular, but saying that they have felt a presence in the house that made them uncomfortable.

The paranormal investigator who recorded the electronic voice phenomenon is convinced that whoever had "spoken" on that recording was expressing anger and pain.

Generally folks assume the spirit is John Henry. They don't think he is there to hurt anybody. He just needs a place to keep on being miserable.

Part Six

THE GULLAH LEGENDS

At several times in the history of the city, Charleston has had more black inhabitants than white. In spite of the many restrictions imposed when the white population began to fear a revolt by slaves and freed men, the black people maintained traditions from their African origins. Their legends and the Gullah language are full of spirits and ghosts. Although originally strictly part of the oral tradition, today their stories are available to us written in everyday English, thanks especially to John Bennett, who searched them out and published them in *Doctor to the Dead,* which first came out in 1946. The book remains a classic. So does Roger Pinckney's *Blues Roots,* published in 2000. A South Carolina native, Pinckney has spent much of his life learning the secrets of the sea islands. The stories that follow are interpretations of stories told by those two authors and other storytellers.

Chapter 21

The Apothecary
and the Mermaid

Peninsula Charleston

This story probably started with an unusually hard rainy season, the kind that leaves folks feeling desperate for sunshine. Charleston was having one like that in the summer of 1867. The story got around the black community that it was raining so relentlessly because a mermaid had been kidnapped, captured in a net by fishermen, and hauled ashore. She'd had a baby in the sea, and, until she was returned to nurse it, the rains would go on. Eliza Burns and Araminta Tucker shared their versions of this story with John Bennett. As with many Gullah stories, the women who told this to John Bennett related it as though they had seen it all themselves. Perhaps they had.

The rain started one morning early in July. At first it seemed to be a normal, seasonal coastal downpour, but it changed into a frightening storm with fierce winds and black skies that didn't stop. After a month, it was still raining. Sometimes the wind blew so hard that the rain appeared to move sideways, from one side of the street to the other, as it came down. This was so abnormal that people began talking about angry spirits punishing the town. The normal elements of a storm—wind, thunder, and lightning—eventually stopped, but the rain did not.

Even in the foul weather, some men tried to keep on fishing, and this reminded local folks that they had seen these same men haul in an unusually heavy net early in the morning of the day it started to rain. Nobody thought much of it at the time, but now, as the rain continued without stopping, a rumor started near the docks that the fishermen had caught a mermaid in the net and, instead of releasing her, had hauled her ashore. She was a new mother and needed to be back in the sea to nurse her baby. That's what the weather was all about: The sea was angry. And the sea would become calm as soon as the mermaid was back in its waters.

As unlikely as the story sounds today, it would have been plausible back then. Legends about mermaids have persisted in areas around the sea where men fish and ships sail. Sometimes the creatures sing and lure men into danger. In this tale, though, the culprit was not the mermaid but the fishermen who captured her.

Day and night, the rain poured down, miring the Lowcountry in mud and puddles and rotting growth. Cockroaches crawled out of their holes and into the streets, where the continuous wash of water drowned them. Dead rats floated up from the swamped wharves. In some places they were still swimming and dangerous, but as they died (which is what happens to rats in a big flood), they piled up in awful, stinking corners. There was no way to escape the swelling water or the stench. In some places water was almost knee-high in the streets, where people had been accustomed to walking and visiting. It soon seeped into the small homes there. There was nowhere to go to get dry or feel safe.

At first people complained. Then they worried. Soon their worry gave way to fear and hysteria after more than a month of steady pouring rain with no sun. The rumors about the mermaid multiplied. One woman started splashing through the flooded streets crying that the rains would not end until whoever had kidnapped the mermaid returned her to the sea.

Afraid that the hysteria would get out of control, the police took the woman into custody, but she just got louder. She screamed that unless they let her out of jail and also sent the mermaid back to the sea to nurse her baby, the sea would come get the captive mermaid. The rain would continue, and the sea would drown the city.

How many times do you have to repeat a claim to make folks believe it? By now the people in the alleys and flooded areas believed. They had flocked to their little churches and prayed, over and over. When nothing got better, they began to feel abandoned by God, or perhaps punished for some sin they could not even imagine. Sometimes they blamed each other for sins committed long in the past. They were scared and fell into the unruliness and irrationality of mob behavior. They swarmed to the waterfront. But they couldn't find anything except muck and bad smells there—no mermaid. Somebody said the foul smell meant the mermaid probably had died somewhere in the area, but a woman in the crowd thought if that were so, the sea would give up and the rain would stop, so she must still be alive somewhere.

Eliza Burns, one of the women who shared the mermaid story with John Bennett, said the waterfront did smell as if something had died there. If it was the mermaid, she said, "they should have exhibited her and charged ten cents apiece to see." They probably could have created some sort of fake display and claimed it was she, which might have calmed the crowd down, but that did not happen. At the time, nobody thought of it, perhaps because it kept on raining. As the people got even more frightened, they headed away from the waterfront, looking for the mermaid in better neighborhoods—or at least for someone to blame for her disappearance.

Even if you wanted to get the mermaid back to the sea, where would you look to find her? Not where the now-empty fishnets hung. Not among the homes and hangouts of normal people. She had to be trapped someplace unusual where odd things happened. Who would have any idea how to keep a mermaid if she wasn't in the ocean?

The apothecary of course. After all, Dr. Trott was not one of them. Who knew what was going on deep in his shop? Dr. Trott probably had her. He might be doing terrible things to the mermaid. An apothecary mixed all sorts of concoctions and potions from mysterious liquids and powders. What if he had made her take something that made her sick or crazy or made her forget her baby? What if he was going to turn her into some kind of medical specimen?

Dr. Trott had in his shop a collection of preserved oddities in jars. Who knew what all? A premature human fetus, a man's misshapen ear, a hand with only three fingers, blobs that looked like little snails. The kinds of ugly things that in later years showed up preserved in formaldehyde at road shows and, even later than that, in some high school science labs, where students gawked with mixed fascination and horror.

Dr. Trott's porter, who delivered the apothecary's potions around town, whispered to some friends that among all those jarred oddities was the figure of a small mermaid, no bigger than a frog. As the story spread through the crowd that Dr. Trott had the mermaid, the part about her being trapped in a jar got lost in the telling. Soon a mob flocked around his shop on King Street, beating on the door, demanding that he set her free.

No matter how strongly Dr. Trott denied having a mermaid anywhere on the premises, the crowd kept at him. They threw rocks and pounded on the windows and door. Somebody yelled that he'd seen the mermaid, trapped in a rain barrel in the basement, crying. But the shop had no basement, so that story died. Somebody else threw a brick into the shop, knocking some of the jars with preserved oddities to the floor and breaking them. Their contents spilled out and, after mixing with all the rainwater, soon disappeared, merging with the dead rats and cockroaches and street muck.

In the heat of the moment, the crowd seemed to forget that the apothecary had provided medicines for most of them, always with positive results. If they could not afford to pay, he gave them the potions anyway and just said, "Pay me when you can." He was a good man, but that was lost in the fear, frustration, and anger of the wet moment. It began to look as though the apothecary was in physical danger. If he were hurt, some of the rioting people would surely regret it later, but nobody was thinking sensibly in the moment.

Seeing a need to quell the potential violence as the mob got more and more out of control, a small group of men, some black, some trusted whites, searched the shop from one end to the other, then climbed onto a low roof to announce that they could assure people there was no mermaid anywhere in the shop. About then, the rain stopped and the sun came out, quickly warming rooftops so that mist rose from them as they dried.

Sun! Glory! People were happy again. But after all the fuss about that mermaid, the one nobody could find to return to the sea, how could they explain that the sun came out anyhow?

A-ha! An inventive person remembered that the mermaid was supposed to be in a jar and said the preserved mermaid had shrunk so much in her bottle that she didn't need the sea anymore; the liquid in the jar was enough for her. That didn't explain the baby that needed its mother, but nobody mentioned it. Some thought that maybe Dr. Trott had taken a moment to carry the bottle outside, where he opened it and released the mermaid into the water so she could return to the sea. Even if anybody did remember the baby, hearing this story about emptying the bottle outside was enough to make them believe everything would be okay.

Either way, the sun had come out, the crowd dispersed, the streets began to dry off, order was restored, and everybody was happy—except, perhaps, Dr. Trott. He moved to a foreign country after the incident. They say he found a place to live inland, far from any body of water, where he gave up his profession, took a modest job in a grocery store, and was never heard from again. There were rumors that he had died shortly after he moved away, but nobody ever found out for sure.

It was a long time before anybody else came to what had been his shop in this little Charleston community, cleaned the place up, repaired the mob's damage, and began dispensing potions once again. When the new apothecary moved in, he expected full payment at the time he handed over his goods. But he did not keep weird specimens in jars, and nobody saw a mermaid in a bottle there ever again.

Chapter 22

The Man Who Would Not Believe He Was Dead

Wadmala Island

Emmy Seabrook told this story to John Bennett, who published it in Doctor to the Dead *in 1946, approximating the black dialect in which Emmy spoke at the time. Here is the story as it might be told today, without the dialect, about a grouchy old man. The older he got, the more irascible he became. No one could tell him anything. As some folks might put it today, "He didn't take telling." After he was dead and buried, he kept coming back, insisting he was not dead.*

His name was Theodore Dinkins, and he lived on Wadmalaw Island. Theodore was old, but the older he got, the more he denied it. He admitted that he had lived a long time, but that didn't make him old. Really, nobody had ever been able to tell him much of anything, and as he aged he got even worse about sticking to his own opinions and beliefs, even when they flew in the face of obvious reality. If someone had told him the sun rose in the morning and set in the evening, he probably would have argued. So he was stubborn about denying his age, even though he was wrinkled and bent, had to sleep a lot, and was often sick. The more his body withered and the more often he was ill, the louder he was in telling folks that he felt wonderful—never better.

He could get up and dance if he really wanted to.

When he couldn't get out of bed anymore, the minister came to see him and, maybe, help him pray for a peaceful home in the next life. But Theodore wasn't having any of it. As Emmy Seabrook told it, he sent the preacher away "with a flea in his ear." Like many Gullah storytellers, Emmy probably told the story claiming to know it was true, because she had seen it with her own eyes. No matter how preposterous the tale, that was often part of the tradition.

Everyone else could see what Theodore wouldn't—that he was going to die soon. His lawyer came to his bedside to try to convince him it was time to make a will. With a cough and a snarl, Theodore sent the lawyer packing, saying in a cranky, raspy voice that when he needed to make a will, he'd talk to a lawyer, but not before.

Pretty soon the doctor came to see Theodore too. "Why are you here?" Theodore sputtered. "There is nothing wrong with me."

"Nothing but old age," the doctor told him. "When people get old they eventually die. And your time is soon."

Theodore roared as loud as his old vocal chords would let him, telling the doctor that he was fine, had never felt better, and certainly was not about to die. A doctor can't do much with an unwilling patient, so he left, knowing the old man would be gone in a day. Of course the doctor was right, and if he indulged in a moment of "told-you-so," who could blame him?

The undertaker came to lay the old man out and put him into his coffin. They carried the coffin to the church, the church bell tolled, mourners gathered, the minister led the burial service, and pallbearers carried the coffin to the gravesite. They lowered the coffin into its grave and covered it with earth, all as usual. People walked away whispering that in the end, death came to Theodore as it does to everyone, no matter how strong the denial. The island would be a little more peaceful now.

But it wasn't.

The very next day, the sexton, who cared for the church and grounds, rang the bell, and dug the graves, showed up early in the morning at the Dinkins's home, looking oddly pale for a black man. "Massa's up again," he told Mrs. Dinkins.

"What do you mean?"

The poor sexton had to tell her that he had seen Theodore sitting on the fence that surrounds the graveyard. He said the old man shouted that he most certainly wasn't dead, he felt wonderful, never better. Calling the sexton a black rascal, he had started to climb down from the fence. The sexton did what any sensible man would do: hightailed it out of there and headed straight to Mrs. Dinkins.

She did not seem all that upset. She probably figured that the sexton had indulged in a little fantasy, as some people do after a funeral, and told him not to worry, just to go on with his daily routines.

But people started seeing the old man on the fence every day. At first it was just island folks. One man came riding by the graveyard on his horse, then slowed to a stop when he saw someone who looked familiar on the fence.

"Is that you, Dinkins?" he called.

"Of course it is," the ghost replied. "Who else would it be?"

"Oh, I heard you'd died and had a proper funeral and burial," the rider said. "Musta been wrong." His horse, sensitive to an unnatural situation, was getting uneasy, so he decided not to stay and chat. As he rode off, he heard a raspy voice yelling something about the rumors of his death being seriously exaggerated, and complaining that nobody stayed to talk to him.

Of course word got around the island. Some people avoided the graveyard. Others went by deliberately to see if there really was an old man on a fence and if it really was Dinkins. Some even stopped to chat with Dinkins, just to see what all the fuss was about. The reports varied. People who live on islands can develop active imaginations if they don't get away sometimes. They have a saying, "Every so often people need to get off the island for a while or they get strange." So just needing to get away could have explained a lot, but then visitors from other places, folks who'd never been to Wadmalaw Island before, began reporting conversations with an old man on a fence by the graveyard.

"He said his name is Theodore Dinkins," one traveling salesman told a store clerk. "He looked a little strange, sort of pale and wasted."

"But that's impossible," the clerk said. "Dinkins is dead. I know. I helped bury him."

For a while the apparition was a novelty, but reported sightings went on for months, eventually annoying islanders who believed that an old man sitting on a graveyard fence insisting he was not dead would be bad for commerce. Finally some of them went to Mrs. Dinkins. "We have to do something," they said. "This is not good for the island. It is bad for business. People will stop coming here if their experiences are too spooky. We can't have a dead man sitting on a fence denying his death and expect anybody to go into our stores to buy anything. We might be used to him, but it's too creepy for strangers."

Mrs. Dinkins listened calmly. She knew Theodore was dead, and she knew that he'd told visitors at his graveyard fence perch to ignore what she said about his death because she never got anything right, including the notion that he was gone. But she'd lived with the argumentative old coot for a long time and had perfect faith in her own judgment. The full burial ceremony of his church and the fact that the will he had eventually written had been probated, dividing his estate and passing it on to his heirs, had not been enough to convince him. Neither had the assembly of mourners at his funeral. She said the only way to shut him up and get him back into the grave where he belonged was to do something so final that even he could not deny it.

They had to bury him again, with much more finality than they'd managed the first time.

It is important to note that nobody was suggesting Dinkins was a bad haint, a person who had been improperly buried and so stayed in this life looking for revenge. That notion applied to prisoners, slaves, or pirates who had been killed and dumped someplace without a proper grave and funeral. Dinkins was just a man who had always been stubborn and would not accept even his own death without an argument.

So volunteers dug his grave again, deeper this time, and placed his coffin back in it. He was in there, they were sure, because the coffin was too heavy to be empty. Then they covered the coffin with even more soil than they'd used the first time. Mrs. Dinkins decided the grave should have a large official stone marker, just to make sure Dinkins got the message that he was dead. Mrs. Dinkins was a smart lady. She knew just how to tickle his ego and, at the same time, prove that he had passed.

Engraved on the stone in big letters were the words: HERE RESTS THE BODY OF THEODORE DINKINS, A HIGHLY RESPECTED NATIVE OF WADMALAW ISLAND. That was to flatter him. Who knows how true it was? The rest of the inscription said, DEPARTED THIS LIFE ON THE SEVENTEENTH DAY OF JANUARY, 1853, IN THE NINETY-FIRST YEAR OF HIS AGE.

And that was emphatic enough to convince Dinkins that, whether he liked it or not, he really had died and properly belonged belowground, not on the graveyard fence. Nobody has seen or heard from him since . . . so far. Never underestimate the power of a woman.

Chapter 23

Don't Let the Boo Hag Ride Ya

A Sea Island

When people around Charleston warn each other about the boo hag, they are not entirely joking. Boo hags are just about the scariest creatures in Gullah folklore. In Gullah belief, people have both a soul and a spirit. After death, the soul leaves the body and goes to the next world, but the spirit remains on earth to take care of loved ones the deceased has left behind—unless it is a bad spirit, or a boo hag. A boo hag always causes harm and misery, robs your energy, and tries to steal your skin.

Young Jimmy was tired, almost too tired to move. He had a good job at the dock, but he couldn't even get out of bed in the morning, let alone work. Once he dragged himself up, it was all he could do to eat a little stew and sit on the porch for a while before he just had to lie down again. Because he lived alone in a tiny cabin and lacked the energy to clean it, the place got dirtier and dirtier. He knew he had to get to a doctor who could fix whatever was wrong with him.

It wasn't a long walk to the doctor's small office at the edge of town, but by the time Jimmy got there, he could barely speak well enough to explain his symptoms. Dr. Mills examined Jimmy thoroughly, and he couldn't find any reasonable explanation for the young man's condition. He asked the usual questions.

"Do you smoke?"

"No."

"Drink a lot of hooch?"

"Never. Don't like it."

"Ordinarily, what do you eat?"

"Rice. Lots of rice. Fish. A rabbit sometimes. Whatever is growing in my gramma's garden."

Well, that diet was better than his own, though the doctor wasn't about to say so. It was close to the end of the day, and since he had no more patients waiting, the doctor took Jimmy home in his rattling old pickup. He promised to bring by a tonic that might help restore Jimmy's usual energy, then headed back to his house in town, puzzling over the unexplained symptoms in an otherwise healthy young man with no bad habits, living a quiet life on the sea island.

The next day, Jimmy's gramma showed up at his cabin to see why he hadn't been around to cut firewood and pick up his basket of vegetables. She was horrified when she saw the condition of Jimmy's home and even more upset when she saw *his* condition.

"Boy, look at you. Why you still in the bed?"

"Too tired to get up," he said. He told her that no matter how long he slept, he woke up exhausted, and it seemed to be getting worse every day.

Gramma wasn't as upset as she had been at first, because by the time he had finished talking, she knew exactly what was wrong.

"Boo hag's been ridin' you," she said.

He had heard of boo hags of course. Everybody had, but he thought they only haunted older people, like the ones he heard complaining about being tired all the time. Honestly, he wasn't really too sure what boo hags were. Gramma, however, was an expert. She told Jimmy that boo hags were undead beings with no skin. They were bright red, with huge blue veins. They looked so awful that the only way they could move among ordinary people was by stealing someone's skin to wear in the daytime. Then, at night, boo hags fly to the chosen victim's home. This gets touchy because, in order to fly, they have to take off the costume of human skin and hide it to put back on later. They also have to pay attention to the time, because if they don't fly back to get into the hidden skin before dawn, they die.

The worst thing about the boo hags (unless you're a human who has lost your skin to one) is that they sneak into a person's house at night. They can get in through the smallest crack, and once inside they find a place to roost until their target is asleep. Then they suck up the person's energy by riding on his chest. The more often that happens, the worse the person feels.

Jimmy wondered how a person could know a boo hag was around, waiting to ride him like that. Gramma said two sure signs were that the air would smell bad, like a dead opossum or fish rotting, and the room would be very hot and damp. That seemed to describe daily life in the area, but Jimmy didn't say anything. When Gramma got going, it was best just to let her keep on. Besides, if the boo hag had already found him and could ride him every night, what he really needed to know was how to get rid of her and keep her from coming back.

The whole time she was talking, Gramma was picking up dirty clothes, putting away dishes, arranging boots and shoes in tidy rows, straightening the bed, wiping the kitchen table, and dusting every piece of furniture in the cabin. Jimmy just sat in whatever room she was cleaning.

The best thing, Gramma said, would be to keep the hag away in the first place. She knew lots of ways to do it. The first was to keep a straw broom upside down near his bed, because boo hags had a compulsion to count small things like pieces of straw. So she found his broom and propped it by the bed.

Some hags could count really fast, though, so it was a good idea for Jimmy to keep his scrub brush nearby too, so that the boo hag would have to stop to count some more. He could hang his sieve near the bed for extra safety. The hag would count the little holes in it. If all that counting took long enough, the hag would have to leave without riding Jimmy to get back to her skin before dawn. Some people, Gramma said, liked to keep an open Bible out because they believed the boo hag would be compelled to read it all from back to front and would run out of riding time before dawn. Gramma decided that this was not an appropriate use for a Bible. Besides, Jimmy did not have one.

Some people cut the posts off their beds so that the boo hag wouldn't have a place to roost, Gramma said, but since Jimmy's bed never did have posts, this one must have found another roost—perhaps a lamp. Then, looking around his little cabin, she said, "Never mind. You don't have to worry about that. The hag probably just slipped in somewhere and never roosted at all." She told Jimmy that boo hags could slip in through tiny cracks in the walls too, but she knew what to do about that. She found the gun he used for hunting, opened one of the shells, and rubbed the powder into a few cracks, then stood the gun next to his bed. Boo hags hated the smell of gunpowder. She said Jimmy would have to paint the window frames indigo blue, because hags couldn't pass through that color. Then, looking at poor Jimmy, she said she would send old Billy over to do that for him.

Just in case none of those measures worked, Gramma put a salt shaker next to Jimmy's bed. "If you salt a boo hag," she said, "it can't get back into its skin, so it dies."

Before Jimmy had time to ask how he could shake salt on a hag if he was asleep and under its spell, she went on to say he would have to act during that period of half-sleep, half-waking when the hag was just getting onto his chest, then reach out and give her a good salting. "Be quick, though," she warned, "because if you struggle without getting salt on the hag, she may decide to steal your skin instead of your energy. You can get more energy, but you've only got the one skin."

Some men say that they've been able to grab a boo hag if their will is strong enough to pull them out of sleep, but most men can't. They say they think they are screaming, but there's no sound. When some strong man does manage to stop a boo hag that way, he will tell you two things: It never comes back, and close up it smells more like raw fish than dead opossum. But of course Gramma wouldn't have known about any of that. Better for Jimmy just to use the protections she had provided.

Just learning all these tricks made Jimmy feel better. He felt lively enough to walk out onto the porch with Gramma and pick up the basket of vegetables she had brought him. He promised to come chop wood for her in a day or two.

As she was leaving, she called over her shoulder, as if she had just thought of one more thing, "You know, Jimmy, you can never tell, the prettiest girl in the world can be a boo hag."

That kind of last-minute comment was a trick she used when she wanted to make a point without seeming too obvious—but, of course, Jimmy knew that. He mumbled, "Okay."

There were some things a guy just didn't talk to his gramma about. He sometimes spent time with Anna, who was just about the sweetest girl he had ever met. Pretty, too. He didn't know how a man was supposed to tell whether or not a woman he liked was a boo hag in disguise. But he didn't want to talk about it right then.

Anyway, she really was leaving now. Her parting words were, "Be sure to keep a fork under your pillow too."

"Why?" Jimmy wanted to know.

Gramma only said it was a trick *everybody* used to scare off boo hags.

So, even though Jimmy had no idea why it should work, he put a fork under his pillow right away.

Then, because he was feeling less tired, he cooked up some rice and some of Gramma's green beans, sliced a ripe 'mater, poured a glass of buttermilk, and ate a nice supper.

It was just after dark when he went to bed with his hand around the salt shaker. He was still holding it when he awoke in the morning. It didn't seem to hold any less salt than it had the night before. He put it down and got out of bed. He felt pretty good.

In the kitchen he heated up a bit of bacon in his iron skillet, fried a potato from Gramma's basket and an egg, sliced another 'mater, poured another glass of buttermilk, and enjoyed a good breakfast. He thought he felt well enough to go back to work but decided to do that tomorrow. Today he would walk over to Gramma's to chop some wood and see what else she could tell him about keeping boo hags away.

The next day, when the doctor stopped by in the evening with the tonic he had prepared for Jimmy, he thought the boy was looking downright sprightly, but he said nothing. He just handed Jimmy the tonic and said, "Only take it when you feel really tired. It will do you more good that way."

Jimmy thanked the doctor, who would not accept payment. Later he poured the tonic into a blue bottle. He kept it on a table by his bed, right next to the salt shaker.

Chapter 24

Jimmy Beats the Plat-Eye

A Sea Island

The plat-eye is another spirit that always means to harm you and has lots of ways to do it. In its natural form, it has one huge red eye in the middle of its head, like a round plate. It has big front teeth and no back teeth at all. But you can't count on that description, because plat-eyes are shape-shifters. They can look like anything from a pig to a huge bear to a mean cat, or even a headless human. Some people can't see them at all, even though they can hear their threatening growls. Plat-eyes are the angry spirits of people who were not properly buried when they died.

It was getting close to dark when Jimmy started walking home. He was uneasy about it because he knew the bad spirits lurked in the woods near his path. Time had just got away from him. After work at the dock, he and some of the other hands had sat on benches near the water, making jokes and waiting for pretty girls to go by. (Jimmy was sorry that wasn't as much fun anymore since his gramma had told him even the sweetest, prettiest girl in the world could still be a boo hag.) Some of the young men had been passing around small bottles of rum, not looking to get drunk, just having a nip together at the end of a hot day. Jimmy kept the bottle they gave him, even though he didn't drink the stuff, because he thought it would be a nice little gift to give the doctor, who did like it, in exchange for the tonic he'd given him to cure exhaustion. Jimmy had not needed the tonic, but just having it there in the blue bottle by the bed reassured him.

But now, approaching the woods at dusk, Jimmy felt almost—well, not afraid, because a fella can't admit to that, but nervous for sure. Gramma had been telling him all about plat-eyes. She knew more about this stuff than anybody, and she said plat-eyes were most likely to show up around the time of a full moon. Jimmy was pretty sure that was tonight.

Plat-eyes were dead people who had never been buried properly, she said. A lot of them were pirates who were beheaded back in the day, or had killed each other and then just got tossed into the ocean or a swamp. That happened up at Battery Point in Charleston, where they hanged a lot of pirates too. Jimmy remembered the old stories about pirate captains who buried their treasure, then killed all their crew so nobody would know where the treasure was, tossed their heads into the hole, covered everything with dirt, and then threw their bodies into the water. Those headless pirates might well be looking for revenge, but it seemed unlikely that any pirate had ever buried any treasure around here, where the cabins were modest, the gardens full of plenty, and the people watchful. Besides, these woods were dense and full of snakes. Surely pirates avoided snakes, didn't they? Jimmy sure hoped so. Pirates could be mean to start with. Meeting up with undead pirates was something it would be better to avoid.

Jimmy walked a little faster as darkness came, in a way wishing it were not a full moon, yet glad for its light to help him see where he was going. He was about halfway home when he thought he heard growling from the woods, but he wasn't sure.

He wished he had in his pocket the "boo daddies" Gramma had once given him. They were good defense against all bad spirits. She had made the charms by tying sulfur and gunpowder together in little burlap pouches. Hers were not the fancy kind made by root doctors, who would use mud, Spanish moss, sweet grass, and salt water, all aged inside a marsh oyster. Then those fancy ones had to be created in the marsh, under a full moon. They could fly to the marsh with no human help. Such "super" boo daddies were supposed to have extra powers, including flying right through solid objects. But Gramma said people in this area did not need such high-powered protection because they lived simple lives. Just keeping one of her boo daddies in a pocket or around his neck would provide plenty of protection.

Well, Jimmy did not have either kind at the moment. A guy just couldn't be wearing boo daddies when he went to work at the dock, so all five of his (one for each pocket and one for his neck) were on the kitchen table at the cabin.

He was almost running when he saw a swirl of mist from the edge of the woods and heard a hideous bellow, a sound he never was able to explain except to say it was like the combination of a bull's snarl and the shriek of a dying hog, which didn't really come close to describing what he had heard.

It seemed better to keep heading for home than to stop or turn around, so that's what Jimmy did. Not much moonlight filtered through the trees on this part of the path, so he had to quit trotting and walk carefully. The sound followed him. So did the swirling mist. And then, off to the side, he saw some kind of creature unlike anything natural that lived in these woods. The shape seemed to have a single, glowing light in the middle of what might be considered its head. The figure started to swell and then kept getting bigger and bigger. Gramma had told Jimmy that a plat-eye had no limit to how big it could grow until it smothered a person in a big, black billow.

Jimmy did not understand why the creature was chasing him, because he had never done anything bad to another person and had never had anything to do with a death or improper burial. Almost before he could even finish the thought, the big, black billow changed again. It turned into a pretty cat with green eyes. Jimmy thought he would have petted it if he had not seen the big monster first and watched it change.

Sometimes, Gramma said, a plat-eye stayed in this half-life to avenge what he felt was an unjust death (like being killed for something he did not do, for instance) or to seek revenge for the wrongful death of someone he cared about. It just didn't seem like anything to do with Jimmy. No way could he help with any avenging. He thought about the doctor, but no one on the island had ever had a bad thing to say about him. He was sympathetic, generous, and moderate in his practices. Most of his patients died of old age, so a plat-eye shouldn't be expecting Jimmy to exact some sort of revenge on the doctor.

As he tried to figure out all the possibilities, Jimmy kept walking as fast as he could toward home. What else could he do?

When he was almost to the end of the wooded part of his path, a new apparition came upon him, still in the woods and still in swirling mist, but close—way too close. This creature looked for all the world like a giant raccoon, as big as a wolf. If it hadn't been for the oddly gold eyes, it would have been kind of pretty.

"Well," Jimmy thought, "if the prettiest girl on the island could be a boo hag, a handsome raccoon probably could be a plat-eye." And it seemed to be edging toward him. In a desperate flash of memory, it came to Jimmy that somebody had told him plat-eyes like whiskey. He remembered a story about a traveler who saw a huge raccoon up in a tree. While the traveler was looking at it, a man came out of a nearby cabin and asked the traveler if he had any whiskey. The raccoon had disappeared at the same time. Too surprised to refuse, the traveler offered the man a drink from the bottle he was carrying. The man from the cabin drained the whole bottle, and then he disappeared too.

People in town said both the raccoon and the man were shapes of the same plat-eye, looking for whiskey. The creatures had a mighty thirst, they said, and a sure way to stop one was to give it a good slurp. Jimmy remembered that bottle of rum he had intended for the doctor. True, rum and whiskey were not exactly the same thing, but maybe one would do as well as the other for a creature of another species who just wanted a drink. He had never heard his gramma say a word on the subject, except to warn him against developing a taste for any of it himself.

Anyhow, he had to take a chance. And with every ounce of courage he had left, Jimmy stopped walking, moved to the edge of the path, scooped out a little hollow near the raccoon, and poured the whole bottle of rum into it. He kept the bottle, though. As the animal started slurping, it started shrinking, smaller and smaller. Jimmy didn't wait to see if it disappeared entirely; he started running. He was almost home.

When he got there, the moon was full, making everything very bright, so he could clearly see Gramma sitting in a rocker on his front porch.

"So, you had an adventure tonight, boy," she said.

How did she *know?*

"I think maybe I saw a plat-eye on the way home," he said. He told her about black creature, the pretty cat, and the raccoon. She kept nodding. Then he told her about stopping the raccoon with the slug of rum he'd been planning to give to the doctor.

"Oh, yeah," she said. "Lots of creatures that like the drink can get lost in the bottle."

He showed her that he still had the empty bottle. "No, that's just a way of talking," she said. "It's what is inside that gets 'em. You were real smart."

She took his boo daddies out of her lap, all five of them, and handed them over. "Remember these the next time, boy," she said. "It will be a whole lot easier."

And as long as he was on the island, Jimmy never went anywhere without Gramma's boo daddies again.

Chapter 25
The Doctor and the Root

A Sea Island

Root doctors could put a hex on someone or remove one— provided the person was a believer. A conjurer's power was said to come from contact with the spirit world. In the old Gullah belief, everyone and everything had a spirit, even rocks and trees and clouds. Some people, often women, used a variety of herbs and roots to protect folks from having a root, or hex, put on them by someone who wished them ill. These women grew and gathered the plants and mixed their "remedies" according to old traditions passed orally from one generation to the next.

Dr. Mills took the cast off little Ella's arm and told her she should be as good as new now, but it would be better if she didn't climb any more trees for a while. Then he looked at her face, a little puzzled. When she was in the office to have her broken arm set, he had noticed a wart near the corner of her eye that he thought would soon interfere with her peripheral vision. He had planned to talk to her mother about removing it, but he realized now that it wasn't there anymore. "Young lady," he said, "what happened to the wart that was growing near your right eye?"

"Oh, Gramma bought it," Ella said. "She gave me a penny for it and told me if I slept with the penny under my pillow, the wart would be gone in the morning, so I did and it was." She tilted her head so he could see directly. She really was a pretty young'un, and she was smiling as if she knew it now.

He told Ella she looked wonderful, and asked if it was Jimmy's gramma that had given her the penny. "Oh, she is Jimmy's," Ella said, "but she's really everybody's gramma. She takes care of all of us. Grown-ups, too." The doctor said good-bye to Ella, told her to stay out of trees for few weeks, and thought that he really wanted to get to know "everybody's gramma." He would ask Jimmy about her next time he came in.

A few days later, at the end of his office hours, Dr. Mills was glad to see Jimmy in his office looking just fine, with no sign of the exhaustion that had overcome him a few months ago. Jimmy gave him another little bottle of rum and apologized for not having brought one the last time. "I had to give it to the plat-eye because I wasn't wearing my boo daddy the night of the full moon," he said apologetically.

By now, statements like this did not surprise the doctor, who was struck, once again, with how nice these Gullah people were and how good working with them had been for him. After his wife, Elizabeth, passed, he had decided to leave his Charleston practice and try something new. Without Liz, Charleston's theater and social life did not interest him anymore. Liz would never have wanted to come to a sea island, but for the doctor it was an interesting new experience and a chance to do some good among islanders who didn't have much in the way of medical care.

But he was discovering that the Gullah folks had a puzzling ability to cure some of their own ills. Oh, they still needed medical help to set broken bones and cure pneumonia and stitch up wounds, but he was amazed at how few people here came to him with some of the ailments that had brought so many people to his Charleston office—headaches, shortness of breath, chronic indigestion, stiff knees, that sort of thing. He realized that something was going on that his own medical education could not explain when he saw Jimmy again not long after the boy had first staggered into his office, too exhausted to do anything. The doctor hadn't been able to find anything wrong and just gave him a tonic for energy. Within a day or so, before the doctor had even delivered the tonic, Jimmy was his old self, working at the dock and sitting on a bench joking with some of the other workers at the end of the day. It wasn't because of anything the doctor had done.

Not long after that, Jimmy brought him a little bottle of rum. Jimmy, who did not care for alcohol at all, wouldn't drink it, but he knew the doctor would. It turned into a regular thing, Jimmy coming to the office at the end of a workday, offering the rum, and then, at the doctor's invitation, staying to chat.

When the doctor asked Jimmy about how he had gotten over his fatigue so suddenly, Jimmy said, "De boo hag was ridin' me, and Gramma taught me how to keep her away."

The doctor said that was good news, but Jimmy looked a little sad. "Gramma says anybody can be a boo hag but you not know. Pretty girl, no matter she be sweet, she could be a boo hag." Jimmy was definitely at the age where girls were an important part of life. This got Dr. Mills to thinking he wanted to talk to Jimmy's gramma about how to tell the good girls from the boo hags. Really, Jimmy needed to know that. So he asked Jimmy to see if he could visit Gramma sometime soon.

It happened that very weekend. Gramma invited him to meet her at church Sunday and come home with her afterwards. The doctor thought this was a Methodist church, but the service was unlike anything he had ever seen in

Charleston. Of course the Lutherans at his church back there were a pretty stolid bunch: no hugging, not too much smiling, formal hymns. Here on the island, the Gullah people worshiped and communed as their ancestors had in Africa, with improvised call-and-response singing. Acting as leader, one of the sisters would sing out a phrase such as, "Do you know Jesus is coming?" and with clapping and stomping, the congregation would respond, "Oh yes, yes, Jesus is coming." It was happy singing, and the doctor found it energizing.

Gramma turned out to be a tiny woman, not much more than five feet tall, with a wide, toothy grin that was too impish to call just a smile. Her curly hair was very short, her skin darker than Jimmy's, all of which emphasized that grin.

She was too involved with the singing and clapping to pay much attention to the doctor until the service was over. After church, he drove Gramma home in his old pickup. She made a fine lunch of fried fish, greens, sweet potatoes, black-eyed peas, and corn bread. He had eaten fancier food, but never any better. After they ate, she gave him that wicked grin, poured each of them a generous slug of dark rum, and they settled in rockers on the front porch.

He said he knew everybody just called her Gramma, but he felt too old to do that. Really, couldn't he use her name? Well, she said, her given name was Elbeth Sadie, "but try saying that and you will see why I'm just Gramma." They struck a compromise. She said the doctor could call her Gramma Sadie. She would just call him Doc.

He asked about the boo daddies she had given Jimmy. She said they were just charms made up of things the haints didn't like, mostly what she grew in her garden and dried. She showed him where her herbs grew—bay leaves, sage, oregano, several fragrant mints. Some people made charms using exotic things such as dried roots, cemetery dirt, bones, and (she grinned again) owls' hearts. They pounded it all into powder to sprinkle around a house or tie into boo daddies.

But all those fancy ingredients really were not necessary, she said. "Where would I get dove's blood? Don't need it anyhow. If a person believes in my boo daddies and potions, they work just fine." She told him sesame oil mixed with cayenne was a good treatment for injuries. Not long ago, a woman had gotten her finger caught in a rope when she was trying to lead a calf to a new pasture and cut off the tip of her finger. She packed it with cayenne powder. It looked awful, but the finger healed and a fingernail grew back. "Nothing magic about that," Gramma Sadie said. "Just a good country remedy."

Finally it was near dark and the doctor was ready to go home before he dared to ask her about Jimmy and boo hags and a boy's natural inclinations and how he might know if he had found a nice young woman who was okay.

That big grin again. "Maybe that scare just slowed him down so he will wait to learn more about a girl before he takes up with her. When he knows her well enough, he'll be able to tell if she is a person who won't hurt him. The day he finds the right girl, not just a pretty one who acts sweet, he'll know." The doctor had known a lot of young men who could have used that advice.

As he was leaving, Gramma Sadie invited him to come again next Sunday. He agreed happily.

The next time they rocked on the porch, she told him more about root doctors. The most famous one was Dr. Buzzard. That was a name he had given himself, part of his showmanship. He was long gone, having died at an old age, though nobody was sure exactly how old he was when he passed because nobody back then kept public records about black people. It might be noted in a Bible somewhere, but who knew where?

Dr. Buzzard wasn't local. He lived up around Beaufort somewhere, but people knew about him all along the coast. Dr. Buzzard always said he got his power when a dove landed on his head. In public he wore glasses with purple lenses. He was famous for his courtroom antics. If someone paid him enough, he could make sure the proceedings turned out in his or her favor by sprinkling a white powder around the courtroom floor.

A judge once said he knew that Dr. Buzzard was trying to root the court and ordered him to stop, but he didn't. He was famous for having given draftees a potion that made their hearts beat irregularly and affected their breathing so much that the military rejected them, sometimes by the busload. Of course that was practicing medicine without a license, giving them something to swallow.

"That would never happen here," Gramma said with a wink.

People had such faith in Dr. Buzzard's powers that they sent him money to work spells on their behalf. The spells must have worked, because he got rich that way. Maybe the most famous story of all, though, was when he climbed into a coffin and ordered it locked, claiming he was so powerful he could escape. When the coffin was opened again, a black cat leapt out.

Gramma laughed out loud, a cackle that matched her grin. "I don't believe that one minute," she said. "But he made lots of money. Whatever he did, it wasn't to help people, it was to make money. It worked because people believed he had the power."

Eventually he died of course. He is buried somewhere, but no one knows where. Anybody who cared about him would have kept it a secret; otherwise people would be digging up his grave to collect his bones as relics. They would be a powerful tool for a root doctor. Just knowing he had them would make people believe in his abilities.

Gramma shrugged. "That's not helping people," she said. "I'm not looking for money. Got everything I need right here. Don't want to be famous. Just want to help people. I don't need purple glasses or anybody's bones to do that."

At the end of one of their Sunday visits, Gramma Sadie gave Doc a boo daddy. "Just in case," she said.

Thinking of all she had said about the power of belief to protect and cure people, Doc remembered a line in the Bible where Jesus healed a man, saying, "Your faith has made you well."

So it was all about belief, Doc thought. He said to Gramma, "Do you think this will do me any good if I don't believe it will?"

Big grin. "If something happens to make you scared enough, you'll believe."

Doc keeps the boo daddy in his pocket all the time. So far, the hag hasn't ridden him, and he hasn't had even a glimpse of a plat-eye.

Appendix A
Seeing the Sights

Chapter by chapter, places to visit on your own. (Note: 800 and 877 phone numbers are toll-free.)

PART ONE: HOSPITALITY HAUNTS

CHAPTER 1: SPOOKY FULL HOUSE

Battery Carriage House Inn
20 South Battery St.
(800) 775-5575
(843) 727-3100
www.batterycarriagehouse.com

It is a good thing ghosts don't take up a lot of space, because Battery Carriage House has a lot of them. If you hope to meet one, ask for room 8 or 10.

CHAPTER 2: GEORGE'S PLAYGROUND

The 1837 Bed and Breakfast
126 Wentworth St.
(877) 723-1837
(843) 723-7166
www.1837bb.com

George, a spunky nine-year-old slave boy who has been dead for more than a century, hangs around here and often plays little tricks to win attention from guests and the staff.

Occasionally someone says the air conditioner is loud, but maybe that's just George.

For a look at a barracoon, like the one where George and his parents might have been kept, check:

The Old Slave Mart Museum
6 Chalmers St.
(843) 958-6467
www.charlestoncity.info

The museum is owned by the City of Charleston and is open Monday to Saturday, 9:00 a.m. to 5:00 p.m. Closed on Thanksgiving Day, Christmas Day, and New Year's Day. Admission is charged.

CHAPTER 3: SPOOKED MANAGERS

Meeting Street Inn
173 Meeting St.
(843) 723-1882
(800) 842-8022
www.meetingstreetinn.com

Jasmine House
64 Hassell St.
(800) 845-7639
(843) 577-5900
www.jasminehouse.com

Between the two of them, these sister inns give their managers lots to do. At Meeting Street Inn, doors are mysteriously locked from the inside when the room is empty, and occasionally an apparition shows up while guests are in bed. Jasmine House was once visited by a mean female spook who tried to keep a businessman from leaving the room. If you book a room here, ask if she has ever returned.

CHAPTER 4: POOR NED PERSISTS

Francis Marion Hotel
387 King St.
(843) 722-0600
www.francismarionhotel.com

Poor Ned was a Yankee who jumped or fell from a room on the tenth floor when he failed to win his love, a Southern belle. Some guests see him; others note that he has opened windows and messed with objects in their room. For the spookiest place, ask for room 1010. The hotel will give you lots of information about the ghost it calls its own.

CHAPTER 5: THE HALF-HEAD CADET

Embassy Suites
337 Meeting St.
(800) 362-2779
(843) 723-6900
www.embassysuites.com

In earlier times, the hotel asked its staff not to discuss the ghost missing the top of his head with guests, but he became so well known that it's okay to talk about him now. Sometimes guests also see what they suppose are Confederate reenactors very early in the morning, only to learn that none have been in the hotel at all. The most active rooms are said to be 105, 231, and the mezzanine room. If you're a smoker, you may want to check whether or not smoking is still allowed in the mezzanine room.

Chapter 6: An Old Woman and a Pooch

Poogan's Porch
72 Queen St.
(843) 577-2337
www.poogansporcoh.com

Mills House Hotel
115 Meeting St.
(843) 577-2400
www.millshouse.com

You might get a glimpse of Zoe, the old woman spirit who seems to resent the place she used to live becoming a restaurant. Little kids stand a better chance of seeing Poogan, the pup that once dominated the porch and is now buried in the yard. The place is known for shrimp and grits and Southern-style biscuits. Open Monday through Friday for lunch, 11:30 a.m. to 2:30 p.m.; dinner 5:00 to 9:30 p.m.; Saturday and Sunday brunch beginning at 9:00 a.m.

If you want to try to spot Zoe without getting too close, you could book a room at the restored historical Mills House Hotel, just a short walk from Poogan's Porch. Although the main entrance is on Meeting Street, one side of the hotel faces Queen Street. On occasion, guests have reported seeing an old woman, apparently locked inside the closed restaurant. If you book here, ask for a room on the Queen Street side.

CHAPTER 7: SPIRITS AND A SPIRIT

Southend Brewery
161 East Bay St.
(843) 853-4677
southendbrewery.com

The ghost here seems to have a split personality. Sometimes guests feel anger and cold spots, but at night when there is live music and salsa dancing, people see a partying ghost. The restaurant and brewery are open Sunday through Thursday, 11:30 a.m. to 10:00 p.m.; Friday and Saturday to 11:00 p.m. The bar is open until 2:00 a.m.

PART TWO: GRAVE HAUNTS

Generally, cemeteries in Charleston are open to visitors in the daytime. For any questions or special arrangements, contact the church offices.

CHAPTER 8: LONELY WOMEN

St. Michael's Episcopal Churchyard
Corner of Meeting and Broad Streets
(843) 723-0603
www.stmichaelschurch.net
Office hours: Monday through Friday, 8:30 a.m. to 4:30 p.m.

Watch here for two wandering spirits whose wedding plans did not work out.

CHAPTER 9: LOVELORN LADIES

The Unitarian Church Graveyard
4 Archdale St.
(843) 723-4617
www.charlestonuu.org
Office hours: Monday through Friday, 8:00 a.m. to 4:00 p.m.

A woman whose husband died while he was far from home and a girl whose father locked her in her room so she could not be with the man she loved are buried here. They sometimes prowl at night, though not together, looking for their men.

CHAPTER 10: GRIEF AND FRIGHT

St. Philip's Episcopal Churchyard
142 High St.
(843) 722-7734
www.stphilipschurchsc.org

Although the graveyard is fenced in and locked after hours, you can still take pictures from outside the fence. This is where a photographer shot a well-known picture that turned out to contain a very clear image of a woman buried here, dressed in white, kneeling at the headstone of her stillborn baby.

The building and graveyard are open to the public Monday through Friday, 10:00 a.m. to 12:00 p.m. and 2:00 to 4:00 p.m.

PART THREE: SCARY PLACES

CHAPTER 11: TOUCH SOMEONE ELSE, NOT ME

Old City Jail
21 Magazine St.
(843) 577-5245
www.nps.gov/nr/travel/charleston/old.htm

This place has an evil feel, as though populated by a lot of angry, mistreated prisoners who, though dead, are still mad. Even some of the tour guides don't much like coming in. The building is now the home of the American College of the Building Arts. The best way to see the place is with a professional tour guide. Tours are also available by appointment if you call the number listed above.

CHAPTER 12: ANGRY SPIRITS

Old Exchange Building and Provost Dungeon
122 East Bay St.
(888) 763-0448
(843) 727-2165
www.oldexchange.org

This dungeon housed everyone from pirates to patriots, most of whom did not survive. The spirits of some may manifest as apparitions, poltergeists, or sounds. Above, in the exchange, important people gathered for major political events. Open daily 9:00 a.m. to 5:00 p.m. Admission is charged.

PART FOUR: HEARD BUT NOT SEEN, SEEN BUT NOT HEARD

CHAPTER 13: THE WHISTLING DOCTOR

59 Church St. and Dueler's Alley

The doctor lived at 59 Church St., where he died. Some people still hear him whistling. The house is a private residence, but you can inspect the plaque featuring an old newspaper article in which the reporter got the doctor's name wrong. You might hear the doctor in Dueler's Alley (really Philadelphia Alley) where he was shot too. The alley is between Cumberland and Queen Streets in the French Quarter.

CHAPTER 14: THE POLTERGEIST PRANKSTERS

Joe E. Berry Residence Hall
College of Charleston
Corner of Calhoun and St. Philip Streets
(843) 953-5507
www.cofc.edu

Several children who died in an orphanage fire still hang around here, even though the orphanage was torn down in 1951. The college dorm was built in 1988 and has been renovated several times since then. The poltergeist kids still sing and set off fire alarms late at night. This place is an all-female dorm and should be treated as a private residence. Visitors can walk the grounds in the daytime, but the ghostly pranks happen long after midnight.

Chapter 15: Strange Encounters

Cooper River Bridge
Ravanel Bridge

Now that the old bridge has been demolished and replaced with the modern Ravanel Bridge, nobody sees the ghost car and its family anymore. It's still a great place to walk or bike, and however you cross it, the views are splendid.

Chapter 16: Gray Man's Warning

Pawley's Island

The best time to see the Gray Man, who warns people on the island about coming storms, is right before a storm—but he really does not want you there then. And given the strength of the hurricanes and tidal surges in Charleston, you don't want to be there anyhow.

Chapter 17: The Silent Scream

The Aiken-Rhett House
48 Elizabeth St.
(843) 723-1159
www.historiccharleston.org/Aiken-Rhett

You probably won't have the experience of the young architects working at the house late at night who saw the reflection a wind-blown woman in the ballroom, screaming with no sound. But check the larger-than-life portrait of Harriet Lowndes Aiken, who stares directly at you as you stand there, looking mad enough to scream. That's scary enough.

The Aiken-Rhett House, operated by the Historic Charleston Foundation as a museum, is an outstanding example of the city's efforts at historic preservation.

Open 10:00 a.m. to 5:00 p.m. Monday through Saturday, 2:00 to 5:00 p.m. Sunday. Admission is charged.

CHAPTER 18: THEATRICAL SPIRITS

Dock Street Theatre
135 Church St.
(843) 577-7183
www.charlestonstage.com

The theater is now home of Charleston Stage, a professional theater in residence. The theater is open Monday through Friday, 10:00 a.m. to 5:00 p.m. Although tourists are usually free to look around, they're not really welcome during rehearsal times. The best place to see the theater's Lady in Red is from the street, looking up at the balcony.

PART FIVE: PLANTATION HAUNTS

CHAPTER 19: GHOSTIES AND GHOSTLY LOVERS

Fenwick Hall Plantation
Johns Island

The Fenwick Mansion is privately owned, and visitors are *not* welcome. However, the rest of the island is being developed, so you can still get some sense of the place by driving around. You probably won't encounter the headless horseman or the grieving girl, but you can see some of area they knew and live oaks similar to the one from which the horseman was hanged.

Chapter 20: The Heartbroken Ghost

Hampton Plantation State Historic Site
1950 Rutledge Rd.
McClellanville
(843) 546-9361
www.discoversouthcarolina.com/stateparks

Open daily from 9:00 a.m. to 6:00 p.m. Mansion tours are available on a changing schedule.

The grounds include gardens and rice fields no longer under cultivation. Watch for a ghostly male figure in the house or wandering the grounds, looking miserable.

PART SIX: THE GULLAH LEGENDS

Chapter 21: The Apothecary and the Mermaid

Peninsula Charleston

Here is a vivid story about how coastal weather can affect crowd behavior. For a really good understanding, walk around the peninsula on a windy, rainy day. This chapter is based on a story retold by John Bennett in the classic *Doctor to the Dead*.

Chapter 22: The Man Who Would Not Believe He Was Dead

Wadmala Island

Another story from John Bennett, this is not about an evil undead spirit—just a stubborn old man who never believed anything anybody told him. His wife figured out a way to put him to rest once and for all. You can visit Wadmala Island to get a sense of what the place was like in an earlier time.

Chapter 23: Don't Let the Boo Hag Ride Ya

A Sea Island

The boo hag concept is so much a part of Charleston lore that it has come into vernacular to suggest spending a totally lazy day in your underwear. According to the original legends, if a boo hag rides you all night you will wake up exhausted. The Gullah concept is developed in Roger Pinckney's *Blue Roots,* an in-depth exploration of African-American folkways of the Gullah people. Pinckney, a native South Carolinian, knows the coastal area and islands intimately. This chapter is developed from his descriptions.

Chapter 24: Jimmy Beats the Plat-Eye

A Sea Island

The plat-eye is another widely known (and sometimes believed) spirit in Lowcountry lore. This creature is an evil shape-shifter who means you harm. Roger Pinckney and several other authors have plat-eye stories.

Chapter 25: The Doctor and the Root

A Sea Island

This story is based on the real experiences of men who have seen and experienced the mingling of Christianity, African rituals, Western medicine, and voodoo, as detailed in Roger Pinckney's book.

POPULAR GHOST TOURS

Personal taste in what makes a good ghost tour varies. Some prefer lots of history, while others want little history but plenty of spooky stories. Some people like them scary, and some don't. Some prefer night tours, while others enjoy getting out and about early in the day. A lot has to do with the guide too. Do you want straight narrative? A storyteller? An actor who changes voices for each character in the story? Would you rather walk or ride? There's an available tour for every taste, because the tour companies are as varied as the individual preferences.

A good way to ensure that you will enjoy a tour is to learn as much as you can about it before you book one. Start by reading the company's description of its offerings. Companies try to describe what they do accurately because they don't want unhappy customers. After you've chosen a tour, it's a good idea to check some online reviews on sites such as Trip Advisor, written by people who have taken the tour that interests you. It's not so much whether they loved it or hated it that will be useful to you; it's *why*. For instance, a reviewer might write that she hated a tour because the guide told off-color jokes, which could be either fun or a turnoff for you.

If you can, ask someone at the tour company for specific information about the guide who will be conducting your tour. Unfortunately, now that reservations are usually made online, telephone calls often end up connected to a recording, but it is still worth a try.

And a final caveat: Make sure you know where the meeting or pickup site is. Get there on time or even a little early, because the tour guide will not wait for you.

The listings that follow have all pleased some customers and annoyed others who did not get what they expected.

Black Cat Tours, LLC
(800) 979-3370
(843) 568-2285
www.blackcattours.com

Tours meet at Market Hall at the Confederate Museum, at the corner of Market and Meeting Streets. Call ahead or check the website for days and hours.

The owners of Black Cat Tours, Mark Jones and his wife, Rebel Sinclair, are professional authors, tour guides, and trained paranormal investigators. They limit group size to twelve people and do not accept small children. Rebel's published books include *The Devil of Charleston* and *Spirit in the Shadows*. Mark has published two volumes of *Wicked Charleston*.

As well as regular evening ghost tours and a Wicked Charleston tour, they offer a weekly free daytime tour of the Battery, to which children are welcome. Mark and Rebel say they named their company Black Cat because Edgar Allan Poe wrote about a black cat, and they have a black cat named Edgar Allan Poe. An alternate explanation, Mark and Rebel say, is that the haunting plat-eye shape-shifters sometimes appear as black cats. Mark and Rebel are members of the League of Energy Materialization and Unexplained phenomena Research (LEMUR).

Bulldog Tours
40 North Market St.
(843) 722-8687
www.bulldogtours.com
Office hours: Monday through Sunday, 9:00 a.m. to 10:00 p.m.

This tour company was founded in 2001 to raise money for the preservation of the Old Exchange. The endeavor has been so successful that the company has gone on to finance the preservation of several more historical sites in Charleston. Most of Bulldog's tour offerings are ghost-related. All tours are at night.

The **Dark Side of Charleston Walking Tour** focuses on Charleston's seedy past—brothels, prostitution, corruption, dirty politics, rumrunners, murder. The tour is not about ghosts specifically, but it does detail events that have resulted in paranormal activity. The narrative is sexually explicit, though laced with history. The tour is limited to ages eighteen and up.

The **Ghost and Dungeon Walking Tour** is the only company tour with nighttime access to the Provost Dungeon.

The **Ghost and Graveyard Tour** features classic stories about grave haunts and is considered family friendly, though managing a baby inclined to cry might be a challenge.

The **Haunted Jail Tour** can be quite disturbing, so it is not recommended for children.

The **Paranormal Investigation Tour** provides an opportunity for you to conduct your own ghost hunt with your own recording devices inside the Old City Jail, with the help of a guide who offers suggestions about how to proceed.

Ghosts of the South Candlelight Ghost Tour
(843) 343-9255
www.charlestonghostsofthesouth.com
Tours leave every night at 8:00 p.m., 9:30 p.m., and 10:00 p.m. from Sheila's Shamrock, 84 North Market St. You do not need to call ahead.

This tour takes you to places where ghostly events have been documented frequently. Some are featured on the History Channel, the Discovery channel, and *Ghost Adventures* on the Travel Channel. Tours stops include a haunted house, a notoriously haunted hotel, and a graveyard, among others.

Gullah Tours
43 John St.
(843)763-7551
www.gullahtours.com
Tour hours: Monday through Friday, 11:00 a.m. and 1:00 p.m.;
Saturday, 11:00 a.m., 1:00 p.m., and 3:00 p.m.

Alphonso Brown leads this two-hour tour aboard a twenty-one-passenger, air-conditioned bus. Brown grew up in a small community south of Charleston and speaks with authority about both the city and the role African Americans played in its development. He knows Charleston's ghosts too. During some of the tour, he speaks to passengers in Gullah, which becomes surprisingly easy to understand once you've heard it for a bit. Some people love this, while others find it annoying. If you are in Charleston during the summer, a tour like this one is a great way to beat the heat.

Holy City Tours
1517 Brookbank Ave.
(843) 860-6808
www.holycitytours.com
Call for days, times, and reservations.

This company advertises "The Best Ghost Tour in Charleston." It also features several "Walks Through History" in addition to the ghost tour. These evening tours leave from the Southend Brewery, 161 East Bay St., third floor. The building is said to be one of the most haunted in Charleston.

Walks in History, LLC
174 East Bay St., Ste. 304
(843) 737-2119

www.walksinhistory.com
Office hours by appointment or chance.

Ed Macy and Geordie Buxton offer a variety of tours based on the books they have written. They emphasize telling "real history" including "grim details" rather than made-up stories or pleasant old legends.

The **City Plantation and Gullah Tour** explores sites and tells their stories as recounted in *Haunted Plantations* by Geordie Buxton. This is a daytime tour. The **Haunted Charleston Tour** is an evening tour based on the book *Haunted Charleston* by Ed Macy and Geordie Buxton. The **Pirate and Haunted History Tour,** based on the book *Haunted Harbor* by Geordie Buxton and Ed Macy, runs during the day and on Friday and Saturday evenings.

HOW ABOUT AN ARMCHAIR TOUR?

The Old Charleston Ghost Shop
168-A Church St.
(843) 722-6877

Here you will find a great selection of books about ghosts, voodoo, and the haunted history of the Lowcountry. You can read about the places you have visited and those you missed and find books about spooky events beyond Charleston. The shop—owned and operated by Stephen Swann and his wife, Maggy—advertises "all things creepy and cool." In addition to books, the shop sells everything from rubber skeletons, magic tricks, and tarot cards to ghost hunting equipment. It's a good place to pick up some dried sage with herbs to ward off bad spirits, too. You don't even have to be in Charleston to visit the store. It's on Facebook and has a website: www.oldcharlestonghostshop.com.

Appendix B

Inside the World of Ghost Hunting

LEARNING THE LANGUAGE OF THE PARANORMAL

As with virtually all specialized activities, the world of the paranormal has some specific language for what you and others experience. Not everybody uses all of these terms, but it is helpful to know them.

Anomaly: Something that deviates from the norm and can't be explained by obvious circumstances.

Benevolent or benign spirits: These terms refer to spirits that mean no harm, such as the gentleman ghost in chapter 1 who just wants to cuddle up with the ladies.

Clairvoyant: This describes people who get information from other than the normal human senses.

Cold spot: A place where the temperature is significantly lower than the rest of a room or building with no obvious explanation. This may indicate the presence of an unseen spirit.

Electronic voice phenomenon (EVP): Voices not heard during an investigation that are captured on a recording. These often require a lot of imagination and interpretation so as not to be dismissed as ambient sound.

False awakening: A person who is dreaming but believes he is awake and reports the experience later as something that "really happened" has experienced a false awakening. This phenomenon may explain quite a few haunted-in-bed stories.

Ghost, spirit, specter, apparition: These words are often used interchangeably to signify the visible presence of a dead person, although sometimes the word "spirit" signifies a presence felt, even if not seen.

Ghost hunt: Going to a place where unexplained events have been reported, but where no one has actually seen a ghost. A ghost hunter tries to record something visible or audible by using video equipment, cameras, and tape recorders to capture a presence.

Ghost investigation: Often initiated at the request of people whose experiences make them believe a site, usually a home or place of business, is haunted. The goal is to explain what is going on.

Haunt, haint, hant: These days, the words are used pretty much interchangeably, but "haunt" would be the proper Charleston term. "Haint" usually refers to Gullah usage, though language purists insist the proper word is "hant" because "haint" is really an old English contraction for "ain't."

Hot spot: A place where the most activity occurs at a haunted site.

Malevolent spirits: There don't seem to be as many of these as there are benign spirits, but people who encounter them have a strong sense that the perceived presence wants to hurt them. Some visitors at the Old City Jail and the Provost Dungeon, as well as some tour guides, report such sensations.

Orb: An unexplained energy, usually white and spherical, that is captured on film, though not necessarily visible to the naked eye. Orbs may also be caused by dust, bugs, or moisture in the atmosphere and are not considered very reliable signs of paranormal activity unless their sightings can be duplicated (with orbs appearing in subsequent photos taken of the same spot).

Poltergeist: Common usage translates the German word as "noisy spirit," but the more accurate translation is "to create a disturbance." The same term is often used to describe phenomena such as the sound of slamming doors as well as instances of objects moving without visible cause. Often the term implies rowdy ghost children.

Residual haunting: This term describes a spirit who died under tragic circumstances and becomes trapped in a recurring loop and reappears over and over without reacting to the present environment.

Residual sound memory haunting: A sound the observer hears that does not fit current surroundings but may be related to an experience a spirit had in the past (e.g., the crack of a whip accompanied by a sense that the stable boy George was in the room at the 1837 Bed and Breakfast).

A Guide to Hunting Ghosts

Eddie Howell is a talented amateur paranormal investigator whose fascination with unexplained phenomena grew from his experiences living in a haunted house. His parents would not talk about or even acknowledge doors that opened and closed by themselves, lights that turned off and on, and strange sounds.

Eddie was beginning to doubt his sanity when the late Nancy Roberts, one of the earlier authors who researched and wrote about legends, mysteries, and ghosts, came to speak at his elementary school. As a result of those early experiences, he and a few friends have made a quiet hobby of investigating reported apparitions and spooky events. Here are his suggestions for beginners interested in similar activities:

1. Never pay other people to take you ghost hunting unless the fee is something like gas or food. There are many free places to go.

2. Never go on private property unless you get permission. You will get arrested.

3. Don't bother people over and over if they do not want someone investigating there.

4. Realize you and your friends are just as important as other seasoned ghost hunters. Your opinions matter, even if the others know more.

5. Don't follow the leader of a big group blindly.

6. Start your own ghost hunting group, and network with others. You'll get into more investigations and make many friends.

7. You don't have to have a big group. Two people are enough, and it is easier to get along with just a few.

8. For equipment, all you really need is a good camera, a digital audio recorder, and a flashlight.

9. Don't pay someone for ghost hunting lessons.

Just watch old episodes of *Ghost Hunters, Ghost Adventures, Paranormal State,* or the online videos of other paranormal investigators. Many people who make money ghost hunting started out by watching such shows and learning by trial and error. Some people have been doing this for a long time. The knowledge they have gained over the years is worth its weight in gold.

10. Have FUN! Ghost hunting should be fun and interesting. If it isn't, don't do it.

Other nonprofessional groups agree with Eddie's suggestions and add some more:

1. Don't just take off after dark to investigate an outdoor site you do not know. Ghosts may come out easily enough at night, but living people who don't know the spot can easily hurt themselves by tripping over a branch or falling into a ditch not immediately visible in the dark. Go first in the daytime, with all the people who will be with you on the hunt. Look for hazards, which could be anything from rusty nails and barbed-wire fences to poison ivy.

2. If you want to investigate a graveyard around Charleston, find out whether or not it is locked at night. Even locked graveyards present possibilities for photographs from the street side of the fence. It is a good idea to let local authorities know if you will be taking pictures in such an area after dark, because these spots may also be meeting places for illicit or illegal activity.

3. Be sure everyone has personal identification, preferably a driver's license with a photograph, to prove their identity. You don't want to end up hunting ghosts in jail.

4. Agree ahead of time who will assume what duties, such as taking pictures, recording sound, writing notes, etc. Designate a spokesperson in case your activities are questioned. This won't be hard if there are only two or three of you.

5. Don't go overboard with fancy equipment if you are just beginning to hunt ghosts. Sheila Turnage, author of *Haunted Inns of the Southeast,* made her ghost hunting tour with a flash camera and a voice-activated tape recorder. Do take extra batteries, though, because many investigators have reported the power from their equipment being abruptly drained at haunted sites.

6. Take a cell phone (or, ideally, have each person in your group bring one). It is your link to the rest of the world if you have problems and, in some cases, can be used for photographing, recording sound, and sending video material. Some phones also allow you to Tweet and post on Facebook. By the time you read this, a phone may be available that will make you pancakes for breakfast. You don't really need that one, though.

7. Tell someone not in the group where you are going and when to expect your return.

8. At the end of your adventure, gather at a designated spot to account for all participants and discuss the experience. Before leaving, some

investigators like to say a quick prayer asking the spirits to stay there and not follow anyone home. Plan to get together back at your home base to discuss the experience at length. Each member of the team may have made different observations and interpretations.

A Selected List of Paranormal Investigators

This is by no means an exhaustive list, but each of these organizations has a solid reputation for scientific procedures and a primary interest in trying to learn what causes the phenomena they have been asked to investigate.

The Atlantic Paranormal Society (TAPS). The organization explains its guiding precepts: "Based in Atlanta Georgia, TAPS was founded in 1990 by Jason Hawes with the sole purpose of helping those experiencing paranormal activity by investigating its claims in a professional and confidential manner, and using the latest in paranormal research equipment and techniques. TAPS brings decades of experience in investigating with its pioneering equipment and techniques that has changed the field of paranormal investigating." This organization does not charge for investigations but does sell some merchandise, such as T-shirts and caps, to raise money to pay for them. The favorite of this author is a T-shirt that reads, DUDE, RUN. TAPS has established what they call a family, or a group of paranormal investigators across the country, who can communicate with each other for advice and to share information. The South Carolina "family member" is the Southern Paranormal Anomaly Research Society (SPARS) in Columbia. (803) 979-3661; http://sparsparanormal.bigfo-rumpro.com/login.

The Ghost Club. If you thought interest in the paranormal was a new trend, check this from the Ghost Club's website: "The Ghost Club is the oldest organisation in the world associated with psychical research. It was founded in 1862 but has its roots in Cambridge University where, in 1855, fellows at Trinity College began to discuss ghosts and psychic phenomena." Charles Dickens was one of its founders. www.ghostclub.org.uk.

Lowcountry Paranormal. This group investigates unexplained activities all along the Southern coast, an area where past hardships explain so many present reports of haunting. Lowcountry Paranormal emphasizes that its interest is in investigation, *not* psychic or spiritual readings. The website has a good guide to taking ghost photographs in daytime and a discussion of the value of electronic voice phenomenon (EVP) recordings. In 2011 the group created a Facebook page. www.lowcountryparanormal.com.

Rocky Mountain Paranormal Research Society. A team of eight that emphasizes impartial research and debunks many reports of ghostly sightings. The team members are of varying ages, with considerable education and professional background. One section on their site, "A look into the world of Photographic problems, Mis-understandings & Hoaxes," illustrated with sample photographs and explanations of how they were created, is both fun and sad. The site has a lengthy list of related books and interviews with some of the authors with a handy "click to order" feature. www .modernparanormal.com.

Appendix C
Who Says?

ANNOTATED BIBLIOGRAPHY

Brown, Alan. *Haunted South Carolina: Ghosts and Strange Phenomena of the Palmetto State*. Mechanicsburg, PA: Stackpole Books, 2010. Alan Brown is a professor of English at the University of West Alabama. He writes about the folklore and ghost stories of the south with a storyteller's knack for entertainment and an academic's care for the history of each event. His stories are brief but include the details as they've been passed from one storyteller to the next.

Brown, Alphonso. *A Gullah Guide to Charleston: Walking Through Black History*. Charleston, SC: The History Press, 2008. Brown's book provides information for finding and visiting such significant sites in black history as Catfish Row, the Old Slave Mart, and the slave quarters of the Aiken-Rhett House. His narrative includes significant information about each place. His company, Gullah Tours, also offers two-hour tours on an air-conditioned bus.

Detzer, David. *Allegiance: Fort Sumter, Charleston, and the Beginning of the Civil War*. New York, San Diego, London: Harcourt, 2001. This is a lengthy, detailed history giving special attention to the six months between Abraham Lincoln's election and the first shot of the Civil War at Fort Sumter. South Carolina was the first state to secede from the Union. Detzer's account focuses on the soldiers, their wives, and the civilians in Charleston at the time.

The book focuses more on human reactions than on broad political issues, setting a scene that seems bound to spawn ghost stories.

Eastman, Margaret Middleton Rivers, and Edward Fitzsimons Good. *Hidden History of Old Charleston.* Charleston, SC: The History Press, 2010. The authors have assembled family stories that have been passed down through generations, often by word of mouth, dating back to early colonial times before Charles Town became Charleston. These stories help illustrate the environment from which ghost stories might emerge. A good example is the chapter "Politics and Pride," with accounts of the first recorded Lowcountry duel and a duel between two Rebel generals following a long and public feud. In light of such history, the tale of the Whistling Doctor seems quite appropriate in a collection of Charleston ghost stories.

Fraser Jr., Walter J. *Charleston, Charleston.* Columbia: The University of South Carolina Press, 1989. Fraser's tome covers Charleston's history, from its beginnings as a British colony through the turmoil of integration into the late 1980s, ending with the massive damage to the city from Hurricane Hugo in fall 1989 and the assurance that Charleston has always survived conflict and natural disaster and will continue to do so. The book is illustrated with old photos, and its massive bibliography includes many unpublished papers. You can find almost any historical place or person mentioned in a Charleston ghost story in this book.

Hall, Lynne L. *South Carolina Ghosts: They Are among Us.* City unknown: Sweetwater Press, 2006. Hall writes that she has been a skeptic on the topic of ghosts, allowing that a city full of hundreds of historic old buildings and cemeteries was bound to spawn ghost stories. Then a personal experience following the death of a person who was important to her softened her stance. This book is written with a sense of play just right for readers who don't take a hard line on actual belief either way.

Harrison, Eliza Cope, ed. *Best Companions: Letters of Eliza Middleton Fisher and Her Mother, Mary Hering Middleton—1839–1846*. Columbia: The University of South Carolina Press, 2001. Many Charleston stories involve women of high social standing. The letters between Mary Hering Middleton and her daughter, Eliza Middleton Fisher (after Eliza married and moved to Philadelphia), give the reader a detailed sense of how such women spent their time. In one telling letter, Eliza recounts a variety of musical activities, socially expected in Charleston, but goes on to say that she will not waltz because it is more interesting to engage in conversation—a stance that might have been more controversial in Charleston.

Keemen, Francis. *Ghostly Encounters*. New York: Warner Books, 2002. In earlier times, the proprietors of inns and hotels said to be haunted tried to keep it a secret for fear of losing business, but that has changed. Keemen has written a guidebook for travelers who *want* to visit haunted inns, hotels, and restaurants. She has written about places to from coast to coast, including Charleston's Battery Carriage House and Poogan's Porch. Each entry includes a brief summary of the site's hauntings and contact information for requesting further information and for making reservations.

Lambreth, Cheralyn. *Haunted Theaters of the Carolinas.* Atglen, PA: Schiffer Publishing, 2009. Lambreth has worked professionally in theater and television and as a paranormal investigator. Her account of Dock Street Theatre reflects her background and her willingness to believe that something unexplained is happening where ghosts are reported.

Macy, Ed, and Geordie Buxton. *Haunted Charleston.* Charleston, SC: Haunted America, a division of The History Press, 2004. The authors observe that the stories in this collection are more grim and historically verified than many of the old ghost stories we turn to for entertainment. This heavily researched book draws material from old records and newspapers. Most of the stories here have not appeared in other collections, and those that have feature more factual information. The sites include the College of Charleston and the Citadel, where violent happenings have been documented. Even the stories for popular sites such as the 1837 Bed and Breakfast go into detail about the nature of life for enslaved Africans and speculate on the connection to reported hauntings. None of the stories carries the "once upon a time" tone of buildings and homes that no longer exist. All the places included in this book can be seen by visitors.

Macy, Edward B., and Julian T. Buxton III. *The Ghosts of Charleston.* New York: Beaufort Books, 2001. In the preface to this book, Buxton writes that as a native of Charleston, he found its ghosts so real he felt obliged to flee to the West Coast lest he be smothered by them. Eventually he came home and found that by embracing what he experienced in his perceptions when he is in Charleston, he could remain there comfortably. He operates Tour Charleston, LLC, with Macy and keeps alive "stories about happenings from Charleston's rich past."

Martin, Margaret Rhett. *Charleston Ghosts.* Columbia: The University of South Carolina Press, 1963. Martin was one of the earliest writers to put ghost stories into print. The *State* newspaper originally published many of the stories in its Sunday supplement. Martin's approach is two-sided. On the one hand, she writes, "I believe in ghosts. I *did* see the ghost at Old House, which is the subject of the first story. I did not dream it." On the other hand, she consulted many old documents and rare books for accurate detail. And when public records and her account differ, she defends the difference by writing that her story is true to the legend. Her work is a classic in the field.

McNeil, W. K. *Ghost Stories from the American South.* Little Rock, AR: August House, 1985. McNeil collected stories that he calls "folklore," to indicate that they have been passed on from one generation to another "orally and, usually, informally." In this context, he writes that traditional stories will change over time and from place to place, until many versions may exist. Also, he notes that distinctions in language make it confusing to know in what form a haunting spirit has appeared. He writes, "Complicating the matter of definition is that the returning dead come back in several forms. First, they may come back in the same body they had while alive; second, they may appear in some sort of spectral form; third, they may be invisible and known only by the deeds, noises or mischief they commit." This is an excellent resource for learning about stories that have been passed on orally rather than in print.

Pickens, Cathy. *Charleston Mysteries: Ghostly Haunts in the Holy City*. Charleston, SC: Haunted America, a division of The History Press, 2007. The first half of Pickens's little book is a walking tour of some of Charleston's haunted sites, complete with street addresses and instructions on where to turn at intersections. She includes very brief accounts of why each place on the tour is notable for its ghosts. The second half of the book, "Charleston's Past—The Intriguing Bits," gives readable, brief accounts of everything from storms and wars to crime and punishment, including the observation that by the 1770s, the city had a tavern for every five men, with only the Methodist Church preaching against alcohol. The book will fit nicely into a purse or pocket, making it a great take-along if you visit Charleston.

Pinckney, Roger. *Blue Roots: An African-American Folk Magic of the Gullah People*. St. Paul, MN: Llewellyn Publications, 2000. Pinckney is a native of the South Carolina Lowcountry. His book, based on years of familiarity with Gullah culture, is a delight to read and a great explanation of many of the relationships between African-American, Christian, medical, and voodoo traditions.

Ressa, Sally and Adam. Interview with the author, May 26, 2012.

Roberts, Nancy. *South Carolina Ghosts*. Columbia: The University of South Carolina Press, 1983. Nancy Roberts (1924–2008) was a model of good storytelling. While her stories were meticulously researched, she did not hesitate to indulge in a little fanciful speculation about their meaning. Over the years she wrote more than two dozen books, most of which have been reprinted many times. She spoke often at schools, involving children not only in spooky stories but also their related history.

Rosen, Robert. *A Short History of Charleston*. Columbia: The University of South Carolina Press, 1992. This is a highly readable and entertaining history of the city, from its beginnings in 1670 as the British colony Charles Town through the period of recovery in the aftermath of Hurricane Hugo, which struck the city in 1989. Rosen is forthright in his discussions of topics some historians tend to soft-pedal: the city's hedonism, early class system, dependence on slavery and its atrocities, and the extreme difference in roles assigned to men and women. (It was a lot more fun to be a man then!)

Rule, Leslie. *When the Ghost Screams*. Kansas City, MO: Andrews McMeel Publishing, 2006. Rule, a professional writer especially interested in ghosts, grew up in a haunted house. This collection of stories from around the country is based on the notion that most ghosts are found in areas of deadly violence. The book also presents another interesting theory: that those who died violently are more apt to remain on earth than people who died a natural death. Rule's mother, the crime writer Ann Rule, suggests in her introduction that ghosts from various periods of time may congregate in an area, with one who comes first and opens a way for others to follow. Some of Leslie's stories are illustrated with her own photographs and include visitor or contact information.

Turnage, Sheila. *Haunted Inns of the Southeast*. Winston-Salem, NC: John F. Blair, Publisher, 2001. Turnage has written about one hundred inns in the Southeast where one might have a paranormal experience. Three are in

Charleston. In a preliminary chapter she offers suggestions for what to take with you to document your experience, if you should have one, and offers the words "spirit," "energy," and "ghost" to describe the phenomena.

Zepke, Terrance. *Best Ghost Tales of South Carolina.* Sarasota, FL: Pineapple Press, Inc., 2004. Zepke has collected some of the state's best-known stories. Her account of events that affected her personally in Battery Carriage House Inn is dramatic. The book includes a down-to-earth guide for conducting a ghost hunt.

ONLINE SOURCES

(Note: All URLs in this section were active at the time of publication unless otherwise noted.)

"The Aiken-Rhett House." Historic Charleston Foundation. www .historiccharleston.org/Visit/Museums/Aiken-Rhett-House-Museum.aspx (accessed 11/13/2012). No longer active.

"Boo Hag." www.urbandictionary.com/define .php?term=boo%20hag (accessed 8/8/2012).

"Boo Hag Legend." http://sciway2.net/2002/b52b/ boohaglegend.html (accessed 10/3/2012).

"The Boo Hags of Gullah Culture." http:// scaresandhauntsofcharleston.wordpress .com/2012/04/22/the-boo-hags-of-gullah-culture (accessed 8/8/2012).

Broach, Jackie R. "Gray Man: Pawleys Island's Local Spirit Is among State's Best Known Ghosts." *Coastal Observer.* www.coastalobserver.com/articles/2012/071912/6.html (accessed 8/20/2012).

"Charleston's Old Jail." www.nps.gov/nr/travel/charleston/old.htm (accessed 8/10/2011).

Ciminel, Bob. "Boo Daddies: Low Country Ghostbusters." www.sitnews.us/BobCiminel/102904_focb.html (accessed 8/12/2012).

"Cold Spots: Poogan's Porch." www.dreadcentral.com/news/32136/cold-spots-poogans-porch (accessed 4/1/2012).

"Cooper River Bridge." www.cooperriverbridge.org (accessed 3/19/2012).

"Dock Street Theatre." www.nps.gov/nr/travel/charleston/doc.htm (accessed 12/6/2011).

"Dock Street Theatre, Charleston's Elusive Darling: Ghosts, Weird Artifacts, Exquisite Art and Fame!" http://shoutaboutcarolina.com/index.php/2010/05/charleston-landmarks-ghost-stories-fun-things-to-do-see (accessed 10/24/2011).

"Embassy Suites Report." www.paranormalinvestigators.com/EmbassySuitesCharleston/embassysuitesreport.htm (accessed 6/28/2012).

"Fenwick Hall Plantation." http://south-carolina-plantations.com/charleston/fenwick-hall.html (accessed 5/16/2012).

Floyd, E. Randall. "Plat-eye Thought to Be Ghost of Deceased." http://chronicle.augusta.com/stories/1996/12/15/met_201329.shtml (accessed 8/11/2012).

Fordham, Damon. "A Port of Entry for Enslaved Africans." www.africanamericancharleston.com/lowcountry.html (accessed 6/5/2012).

Francis Marion Hotel, "Our Ghost Story." www.facebook
.com/note.php?note_id=10150388886048249 (accessed
8/3/2012).

Ghost Hunting 101. www.ghosthunting101.com (accessed
6/5/2012).

"The Ghosts of Charleston." www.visitcharleston.org/ghosts
.htm (accessed 10/3/2012).

"Ghost of the Whistling Doctor." www.charlestonfootprints
.com/charleston-blog/ghost-of-the-whistling-
doctor-3/2011/08/09 (accessed 4/23/2012).

"The Gray Man." www.hauntedlowcountry.com/index.php?/
hauntlow/south_carolina (accessed 8/12/2012).

Hambrick, Greg. "Ghost Hunting at Charleston's Old
Jail." www.charlestoncitypaper.com/charleston/ghost-
hunting-at-charlestons-old-jail/Content?oid=1111195
(accessed 1/20/2012).

"Hampton Plantation EVP." www.angelsghosts.com/
hampton_plantation_evp_recording.html (accessed
8/17/2012).

Hastie, Drayton. "Charleston Ghost Stories at Battery
Carriage House Inn." www.batterycarriagehouse.com/
ghosts.htm (accessed 10/25/2011).

Lewis, Fairweather. "Vanishing Vehicles." http://
fairweatherlewis.wordpress.com/2010/05/16/vanishing-
vehicles (accessed 3/19/2012).

McKinney, Wanda. "Haunted Charleston Walking Tour."
Southern Living. www.southernliving.com/travel/south-
east/haunted-charleston-walking-tour-00400000009303
(accessed 1/30/2012).

"Old Exchange Building & Provost Dungeon History." http://oldexchange.org/history (accessed 3/12/2012).

"Old Slave Mart." www.charlestonlowcountry.com/about/ slaveMart.html (accessed 7/13/2012)

"The Plat Eye." http://themoonlitroad.com/the-plat-eye (accessed 8/11/2012).

"Plat-eye." www.monstropedia.org/index.php?title=Plat- eye#See_Also (accessed 8/3/2012).

"Poogan's Porch: A New Story." http://ghosttakers.com/ poogan's_porch.htm (accessed 4/19/2012).

"Praising Charleston: The Honeymoon Hotel." http:// photodude.com/2002/11/04/praising-charleston-the- honeymoon-hotel (accessed 7/30/2012).

"Provost Dungeon, Charleston, SC." www.castleofspirits .com/stories05/provos.html (accessed 3/12/2012).

"Provost Dungeon." www.graveaddiction.com/duncharl .html (accessed 2/14/2012).

Reinbold-Gee, Shannon. "Charleston, South Carolina." www .realhaunts.com/united-states/the-battery (accessed 9/9/2012).

Ross, L. Woodrow. "Ghosts of South Carolina: Two Stories of Lost Love and Traffic Death." www.independentmail .com/news/may/21/ghosts-south-carolina-two-stories- lost-love-and-tr (accessed 8/17/2012). No longer active.

Simmel, Caroline. "Petitioned College of Charleston: Refund Housing Tuition for Residents of Joe E. Berry Hall." www.change.org/petitions/college-of-charleston- refund-housing-tuition-for-residents-of-joe-e-berry-hall (accessed 8/24/2012).

Smith, Glenn. "Phantoms of the Playhouse." *The Post and Courier.* www.postandcourier.com/article/20081031/PC1602/310319908 (accessed 10/3/2012).

Southend Brewery. "Our Ghosts." http://southendbrewery.com/about-restaurant-bar-charleston-sc/our-ghost-story (accessed 5/11/2012).

St-Laurent, Carole. "Haunted Charleston." http://romancebeyond.com/general/haunted-charleston (accessed 8/24/2012).

Stonestreet, O. C. "Pawleys Island and the Ghostly Legend of the Gray Man." www2.mooresvilletribune.com/news/2010/jul/18/pawleys-island-and-ghostly-legend-gray-man-ar-307271 (accessed 10/3/2012).

"A Stroll Down 'Dueler's Alley.'" http://charlestongateway.com/features/a-stroll-down-duelers-alley (accessed 4/23/2012).

Treadwell, Jaine. "All about Haints." www.troymessenger.com/2009/09/25/all-about-haints (accessed 10/24/2011).

Warren, Joshua. "Report on Investigation of the Charleston, SC Old City Jail." http://shadowboxent.brinkster.net/LEMUR/charlestonoldcityjail.html (accessed 1/20/2012).

About the Author

Sara Pitzer has been traveling in and writing about the Southeast since 1983. She is the author of *North Carolina Off the Beaten Path* and *Myths and Mysteries of North Carolina,* both published by Globe Pequot Press. Although Sara has stayed in many Charleston B&Bs, eaten enough Lowcountry food to need a low-cal diet, visited museums and plantations, and walked through graveyards, she has never seen a ghost. And that's quite okay with her.